IMAGES OF WAR

ARMOURED WARFARE

IN THE
BATTLE FOR NORMANDY

The most common type of panzer deployed to Normandy was the Panzer Mk IV Ausf H and Ausf J. Rommel had almost 750 of these tanks as his disposal and they could easily outshoot the American M4 Sherman. This Panzer IV belonged to the 3rd Panzer Regiment, which was one of the 2nd Panzer Division's tank units; it was knocked out at Pont-Farcy. (*US Army/NARA*)

IMAGES OF WAR

ARMOURED WARFARE

IN THE
BATTLE FOR NORMANDY

RARE PHOTOGRAPHS FROM
WARTIME ARCHIVES

ANTHONY TUCKER-JONES

Pen & Sword
MILITARY

First published in Great Britain in 2012 by
PEN & SWORD MILITARY
an imprint of
Pen & Sword Books Ltd,
47 Church Street,
Barnsley,
South Yorkshire.
S70 2AS

A CIP record for this book is available from the British Library.

ISBN 978 184884 517 6

Typeset by Chic Media Ltd

Printed and bound by CPI Group (UK) Ltd., Croydon, CR0 4YY

Pen & Sword Books Ltd incorporates the Imprints of
Pen & Sword Aviation, Pen & Sword Maritime, Pen & Sword Military,
Wharncliffe Local History, Pen & Sword Select, Pen & Sword Military
Classics, Leo Cooper, Remember When, Seaforth Publishing and
Frontline Publishing.

For a complete list of Pen & Sword titles please contact
Pen & Sword Books Limited
47 Church Street, Barnsley, South Yorkshire, S70 2AS, England
E-mail: enquiries@pen-and-sword.co.uk
Website: www.pen-and-sword.co.uk

Contents

Introduction

The Americans, British, French, Canadians and Poles were to commit a total of thirteen armoured divisions and numerous independent armoured brigades to the battle for Normandy. This battlefield was very different to the wide-open spaces of the deserts of North Africa and the sweeping steppe of the Eastern Front. Both sides found themselves engaged in bitter battles amidst Normandy's fields, orchards and cities. Initially the anticipated mobile armoured warfare did not materialise as the Allies were hemmed in at their bridgehead. Instead there was a brutal slogging match in which the Allies were forced to trade their superior resources with the battle-hardened panzers in an effort to secure first Cherbourg and turn the German flank either side of Caen. The latter in the British and Canadian sector become the lynchpin of the whole battle, because beyond it lay open tank country.

The D-Day Landings on 6 June 1944 presented Allied military planners with a unique set of problems when it came to liberating Nazi-occupied France. They had to not only successfully ferry their armoured forces across the English Channel and overcome German coastal defences, but also fend off and then defeat the inevitable counter-attack by Adolf Hitler's panzers. The Dieppe raid in 1942 had shown how not to do it: attempting to seize and hold a French port had resulted in Allied tanks becoming trapped in the town. Instead it was decided to assault the open beaches of the Normandy coastline.

A major concern were the beach obstacles in the selected landing zones, which posed a threat to the smaller assault craft. These consisted of steel and wooden posts, many of which had mines attached, capable of tearing a craft's hull open. The Navy conducted various experiments to determine their effect on the different types of landing craft; General Hobart's 79th Armoured Division, which operated the specialised assault vehicles known as the 'Funnies', was given the task of clearing the way and breaking though the 'crust' of Hitler's 'Fortress Europe'.

After the Allied landings in the Mediterranean during 1942–43, Hitler was anticipating landings in northern France and intended inflicting a bloody reverse. By mid-1944 about one fifth of his field army was occupying western Europe. Field Marshal von Rundstedt, Commander-in-Chief West, had well over half a million men guarding the European coastline, with about fifty-eight divisions stationed in France and the Low Countries. They were divided into two Army Groups with a Panzer Group of about ten armoured divisions poised to crush any landings.

Field Marshal Rommel, who took command of Army Group B in February 1944, wanted the panzers well forward to deal with the Allies as soon as they came ashore. He had witnessed Allied tactical air strikes in North Africa and knew that if they held their tanks back they would struggle to reach the battle unmolested. Rundstedt on the other hand favoured the 'crust-cushion-hammer' concept, the crust being the static sea defences, the cushion the infantry reserves and the hammer the panzers held in reserve. A messy compromise resulted in half the panzers being held as a strategic reserve, with control ultimately resting with Hitler.

Hitler was convinced that Normandy was not the main invasion point. He was aided in this delusion by Allied deception plans, the bombing of Calais and the disruption of the northern French rail system. An American ghost army in northern England had convinced him that they were going to land north of the Seine, and as a result numerous German divisions, especially armoured, remained beyond the Seine for up to a week after D-Day.

Hitler only had eight divisions engaged during the first six weeks of the campaign; the Allies were expecting at least twice as many. More and more German units were eventually drawn into the battle and by the end of June facing the British were approximately 725 panzers, while on the American front there were only 140. The desperately needed German infantry divisions that could free up their armour for a massed counter-attack remained north of the Seine.

Following the American breakout, even as part of Army Group B was being overwhelmed in the Falaise pocket, far to the south the Americans were in a headlong rush toward the Seine to trap even more German forces. It seemed as if Hitler's generals were on the verge of a second, much bigger, disaster. Unfortunately determined resistance held up the Americans as the retreating troops fought desperate rearguard actions along the Seine. After the Falaise pocket had been overrun Field Marshal Model conducted a highly successful rearguard operation at Rouen, saving the survivors of his exhausted and scattered command.

The situation appeared irretrievable for Hitler: while he had barely 100 serviceable panzers, the Allies could muster almost 8,000 tanks. It seemed as if nothing would stop their armoured juggernaut and by 4 September 1944 they were 200 miles east of the Seine and in control of the vital port of Antwerp. However, while the Allies had won the battle for Normandy, crucially many of Hitler's panzer troops escaped to fight another day.

Photograph Sources

The dramatic images in this volume have been drawn principally from those taken by the American combat photographers who served with the US Army's Signal Corps in Normandy: these are now held by the US National Archives and Records Administration (NARA) and the quality of the photographers' work speaks for itself.

Other images are also drawn from those taken by the film unit with the Canadian Army in Normandy and held by the Canadian National Archives, the French Normandie Mémoire Collection and the author's own collection (resulting in part from his earlier Normandy work, *Falaise: The Flawed Victory* published by Pen & Sword) built up over the last thirty years from a wide variety of sources.

Lastly the author is indebted to a number of individuals who were kind enough to share their private collections and offer their expertise, including Alan Jones. Picture editing is a very subjective art and the final selection in this book rests with the author – he hopes that readers enjoy them.

This book is dedicated to Typhoon pilot Flight Lieutenant Godfrey 'Wimpey' Jones, 181 Squadron, who was killed in action over Caen on 16 June 1944 whilst attacking the panzers.

Chapter One

Panzergruppe West

Adolf Hitler mustered ten panzer divisions and one panzergrenadier division in Nazi-occupied Normandy in 1944, totalling 160,000 men equipped with just over 1,800 panzers. In addition he had another dozen or so General Headquarters panzer formations, mainly of battalion strength, with a further 460 panzers. This gave Hitler's Army Group B (7th Army, Panzergruppe West and the various panzer corps commands) an accumulated strength of around 2,260 tanks with which to fend off Operation Overlord on 6 June 1944.

Field Marshal Erwin Rommel, commanding Army Group B, wanted his panzers well forward to deal with the Allies as soon as they waded ashore. Rommel, who had made his name as a panzer commander in France and North Africa, knew only too well how potent Allied air power could be, which is partly why he advocated keeping the panzers near the coast. He did not reckon with the Allies' heavy naval gunfire, however, which would greatly hamper the panzers even when they did get near the beachhead.

General Geyr von Schweppenburg, Commander Panzergruppe West, was dismissive of Rommel's urge to strike the Allies on the beaches. He seemed aware that this would expose them to concentrated naval gunfire and fighter-bombers; in addition his existing forces were insufficient and vital fuel and ammunition stocks lay too far to the rear to assist rapid deployment. He preferred drawing the Allies inland first before striking. The net result was an unwieldy compromise that benefited no one but the Allies on D-Day.

The one major advantage that the Germans had was the qualitative edge of their panzers. Hitler realised they could never match the Allies' numbers but he ensured that they could outshoot them. On the whole the German armour deployed in northern France in 1944 was vastly superior to that of the Allies.

The most common type of panzer in Normandy – with a total of 748 tanks – was the Panzer Mk IV Ausf H and Ausf J, which went into production in 1943 and 1944 respectively. Its gun had a 20 per cent greater muzzle velocity than that of the American-built M4 Sherman's 75mm gun, meaning that it could punch through 92mm of armour at 500 yards, while the Sherman could only manage 68mm. With frontal armour of 80mm and a 75mm KwK 40 L/48 anti-tank gun this model provided the backbone of the German panzer divisions.

Normally the Panzer IV was allocated to the 2nd battalion of a panzer regiment, although there were a number of exceptions. The 1st battalion of the 9th Panzer Division's Panzer Regiment 33 was equipped with Panzer IVs and both battalions of 21st Panzer Division's Panzer Regiment 22 were equipped with it.

Another common armoured fighting vehicle in Normandy was the Sturmgeschütz or StuG III assault gun armed with the 75mm StuK 40 L/48, and to a lesser extent the StuG IV equipped with the same weapon, which was used to equip the tank-destroyer battalions of the panzer divisions and in some cases substituted for the Panzer IV. They also equipped the independent Sturmgeschütz Brigades, a number of which were deployed throughout France. Lacking a turret, this assault gun was a very good defensive weapon and ideally suited for the Normandy countryside.

While the Tiger's technological excellence meant it took twice as long to build as the Panther, its gun could easily deal with every single type of Allied tank. Many Allied tank crews were soon to develop 'Tiger anxiety' and for good reason. The Tiger could tear a Sherman tank apart, while the latter's gun could not penetrate the Tiger's frontal armour. The American 75mm gun could only pierce the Tiger at close range and while the British 17-pounder gun was much more effective it was not available in significant numbers. Even those Shermans armed with a 76mm gun had to close to 300 yards to be effective. However, while the Tiger I was a formidable weapon with 100mm frontal armour and an 88mm KwK L/56 gun, only three battalions were deployed in Normandy, with about 126 tanks.

Similarly the Tiger II (or King Tiger/Royal Tiger) was brand new in June 1944, but only one company was equipped with them, totalling about a dozen tanks in Normandy. In many ways its high fuel consumption, limited operational range, fragile steering and slow turret traverse nullified its powerful main armament, the 88mm KwK 43 L/71, and very thick armour.

While they remained in range, naval fire support from the Allies' warships in the channel produced the most devastating results against the massing panzers. The one thing that the Tiger crews feared was naval gunfire as this delivered the heaviest shells, which could flip a tank right over – on one occasion trapping the crew for several hours before they could be dug free.

The Panzer Mk V, or Panther, represented the pinnacle of German tank production, mounting the powerful 75mm KwK 42 L/70 gun that could penetrate 120mm of armour at 1,094 yards. The main models deployed in Normandy were the Ausf A and Ausf G. Theoretically each 1st battalion of a panzer regiment was equipped with this tank. On the Eastern Front it had proved itself superior to the Soviet T-34, though mechanical teething problems initially rendered it unreliable.

The Jagdpanzer IV, mounting the same gun as the Panther, was intended as a StuG replacement but was never built in sufficient numbers. It also appeared in 1944 and began to replace the Marder self-propelled gun in the panzer divisions' tank-destroyer battalions. Only about sixty were deployed in Normandy. Similarly the Jagdpanther, based on the Panther chassis and armed with the 88mm PaK 43/3, were few in number in Normandy, about a dozen at the most.

The main self-propelled anti-tank weapon was the Marder, armed with a 75mm PaK 40/3. The principal self-propelled artillery in Normandy comprised the Hummel self-propelled 150mm howitzer, based on the Panzer IV chassis, and the Wespe based on the Panzer II, armed with a 105mm gun. The Germans also deployed a range of hybrid self-propelled guns based on French tank and ammunition tractor chassis.

It did not take long for Schweppenburg to realise just how vulnerable the German Army was; naval gunfire, artillery and aircraft caused excessive casualties, hindered movement and were a drain on morale. In particular the panzer divisions were under threat from rapid attrition, especially as replacements were not forthcoming. Allied naval gunfire also impeded the movement of supplies, particularly ammunition, and local dumps were quickly exhausted, forcing vulnerable motor vehicles to forage further afield, exposing them to air attack.

After his desert experiences Rommel perhaps overestimated the effects of the Allies' fighter-bombers. In Normandy the sustained and often heavy attacks by the Allied bombers and fighter-bombers produced surprisingly mixed results against the armoured fighting vehicles of Panzergruppe West and the 7th Army. In fact the bomber raids preceding the Allies' major offensives often proved more fatal to their own men and hindered the advance because of the damage caused.

Rockets and free-fall bombs were highly inaccurate when trying to hit vehicles and the Germans were masters of camouflage. The Allied air forces' real contribution was the sense of panic that their attacks caused; vehicle crews quickly took to the fields at the onset of an air strike; their vehicles, though, often remained unscathed.

By the end of June 1944 it was evident that Army Group B's 'crust-cushion-hammer' (sea defences-infantry-panzers) tactics had failed despite the slowly increasing number of panzer divisions; in the face of Allied firepower and attacks, the tied-down panzers could do little more than fire-fight as the situation developed.

The desperately needed German infantry divisions that should have freed up the panzers for a counter-stroke remained north of the Seine. Hitler held them back because he feared an attack across the Pas de Calais; this left the panzers in a largely static role. To make matters worse, by the beginning of July the unrelenting operational commitment meant that 58 per cent of the Panthers and 42 per cent of the Panzer IVs were in the maintenance depots.

Field Marshal Gerd von Rundstedt, Commander-in-Chief West, seen here on the right, favoured the 'crust-cushion-hammer' strategy, in which the panzers were held back as the hammer to strike the Allies once they had landed in France. (*Author's Collection*)

In contrast the very able Field Marshal Erwin Rommel, commanding Army Group B in western France, was at loggerheads with his boss von Rundstedt and General von Schweppenburg, the commander of Panzergruppe West. Rommel knew that if the panzers were kept too far back they would struggle to reach the beaches in the face of Allied air power. (*US Army/NARA*)

A row of captured German PaK 40 75mm anti-tank guns; the Germans had this weapon in abundance in Normandy. (*US Army/NARA*)

General Josef 'Sepp' Dietrich, seen here, commaded 1st SS Panzer Corps; two such Waffen-SS Panzer Corps were to play a key role in the battles for Normandy. (*Author's collection*)

Curious American GIs examine a Panzer Mk V or Panther at le Désert, north of St Lô – they do not seem to have been put off by the charred remains of the Panzertruppen lying on the back. This tank belonged to the Panzer Lehr Division and may have been knocked out during the division's counter-attack on 11 July 1944. Most of the Panther units deployed to counter the Allied invasion of France in mid-1944 were the Panther Ausf A (somewhat confusingly the second production model – the versions ran: Ausf D, A and then G). About 2,000 of these were built between August 1943 and May 1944. (*US Army/NARA*)

The first shot shows members of the 101st SS Heavy Tank Battalion with their camouflaged Tiger Ausf E. This was reportedly taken just after their successful clash with the British 22nd Armoured Brigade (7th Armoured Division) at Villers-Bocage on 15 June 1944. While the Panzer Mk VI Tiger earned a reputation as a tank killer par excellence thanks to its thick armour and powerful 88mm gun, it was never available in sufficient numbers; in all, Panzergruppe West had about 130 available in Normandy. This second tank seems to have been abandoned at the roadside. (*Author's Collection*)

Another common armoured fighting vehicle in Normandy was the Sturmgeschütz III 40 Ausf G. This highly successful assault gun was produced from December 1942 until March 1945. While it was equipped with a 75mm gun, some StuG detachments were also supplied with the Sturmhaubitze variant armed with a 105mm howitzer. (*US Army/NARA*)

The main type of German self-propelled artillery in Normandy comprised the Wespe (seen here) utilising the Panzer Mk II chassis armed with a 105mm and the Hummel using the Panzer Mk IV chassis with a 150mm gun. Wespe were issued to the self-propelled detachments of the panzer artillery regiments in both the panzer and panzergrenadier divisions. (*US Army/NARA*)

Panzerjäger self-propelled detachments of both the panzer and infantry divisions were issued with the Panzerjäger 38(t). This particular example is trying to avoid the attentions of Allied fighter-bombers in Normandy. (*Author's Collection*)

Another use for the Czech 38(t) chassis was as a flakpanzer (anti-aircraft tank) mounting a 20mm Flak 38 L/55 anti-aircraft gun. It was issued in early 1944 to the AA platoon of each tank regiment in the panzer divisions stationed in the West and saw considerable service in Normandy. This example has clearly changed hands and is now the property of the US Army. (*US Army/NARA*)

American troops examining captured French Renault tanks. The Germans fielded a number of captured French tanks and hybrid self-propelled anti-tank guns with the 21st Panzer Division (reformed after its loss in North Africa), Training and Replacement Battalion 100 and Panzer Battalion 206. (*Author's Collection*)

This abandoned self-propelled gun is a Renault R-35 chassis fitted with a Czech 47mm anti-tank gun. Only 174 of these conversions were made in 1941 – clearly a few saw action in Normandy, with the panzerjäger units. Easily outgunned, such vehicles did not last long. (*US Army/NARA*)

This rather strange-looking tracked vehicle is a remote-controlled Goliath Sd Kfz 302, which could deliver a 60kg charge. The 2nd Panzer and Panzer Lehr Divisions each had a remote-controlled demolition company. They also deployed the manned Sd Kfz 301, which could carry 500kg of explosives. (*US Army/NARA*)

Captured German weaponry: there are PaK 40s on the right, and of note in the middle is the 105mm leFH18 the standard divisional field piece, while on the left is the heavier sFH18 150mm howitzer. (*US Army/NARA*)

This small infantry support weapon is a Raketenwerfer 43 anti-tank gun. In the second photo in the background are its larger cousins: a PaK 38 50mm and a PaK 43/41 88mm anti-tank gun. (*US Army/NARA*)

The Raketenpanzerbuchse was better known as the Panzerschreck or 'Tank Terror'. This was based on the American M1A1 'Bazooka' 2.36in rocket launcher, which had fallen into German hands following the Allied landings in French North Africa in November 1942. The Panzerschreck along with the smaller Panzerfaust were the Germans' main hand-held anti-tank weapons in Normandy – both were weapons that Allied 'tankers' greatly feared. (US Army/NARA)

GIs familiarise themselves with German-, French- and Russian-made hand grenades; to the left are German Teller anti-tank mines. (*US Army/NARA*)

As well as 105mm and 150mm artillery, fire support was also provided by the Wurfrahmen and Nebelwerfer rocket launchers, the former were fitted to half-tracks and munitions carriers. (*US Army/NARA*)

While the German Army had a reputation for being fully mechanised, in fact it still relied heavily on horses for transport and to pull artillery and field kitchens. (*Scott Pick Collection*)

US paratroops take a ride through Carentan on a captured Kübelwagen Sd Kfz 1. This served a similar function to the ubiquitous American utility jeep in both the panzer and infantry divisions. It was a very common vehicle within the German armed forces, with some 52,000 produced by the end of the war. (*US Army/NARA*)

Chapter Two

Normandy Bound

The Allies (Americans, British, French, Canadians and Poles) deployed thirteen armoured divisions and multiple independent armoured brigades to the battle for Normandy. Their accumulated strength for the campaign amounted to almost 8,700 tanks. Two-thirds of those used by the British, Canadian and Polish armoured units in Normandy were the ubiquitous Sherman, the rest being mainly British-built Cromwell and Churchill tanks.

Therefore easily the most common Allied tank to fight in Normandy was the American M4 and M4A1 Sherman. While mechanically reliable, it was handicapped by thin armour and a gun lacking sufficient punch. Its good cross-country speed and higher rate of fire could not make up for these two key shortcomings. Tank crew survival was paramount – tanks could be replaced relatively easily but not experienced crews. However, the Sherman had a nasty habit of burning when hit and, if this happened, the crew only had a 50 per cent chance of survival.

The Americans developed tank destroyers based on the Sherman that could penetrate at least 80mm of armour at 1,000 yards, notably the M10 Wolverine armed with a 3-inch gun and the M36 armed with a 90mm gun, but there were not enough of them. The 3-inch gun was intended to tackle the Tiger, but since it could only penetrate the frontal armour at 50 yards it was all but ineffective against this panzer. Similarly the M18 Hellcat, armed with a powerful 76mm gun, was not available in sufficient numbers.

The British Cromwell cruiser tank was numerically and qualitatively the most significant British tank and, along with the Sherman, formed the main strength of the British armoured divisions. However, even armed with a 75mm gun it was inferior to the later model Panzer IVs and the Panther. Although fast, the narrowness of the hull made up-gunning it very difficult. Similarly the British Churchill infantry tank, though heavily armoured, could not take any gun larger than the 75mm.

The heaviest British weapon – the 17-pounder (76.2mm) – could open up 120mm of armour at 500 yards and was either towed or mounted in a limited numbers of Shermans, designated the Firefly VC. Later it was also mounted in the Valentine chassis, creating the unwieldy Archer self-propelled gun, and in the M10 to create the British Achilles, though these did not enter service until well after the Normandy campaign. The Sherman Firefly was the only Allied tank capable of taking on the Panther and the Tiger on equal terms, but due to the shortage of guns only one was issued per troop. As a result the Allies' tanks experienced a severe mauling at the hands of the panzers for three months.

The key craft for getting the tanks ashore was the Landing Ship Tank (LST), which was capable of carrying sixty vehicles or 300 troops. In total 1,051 of these were built during the Second World War, seeing action in the Mediterranean, Pacific and the English Channel. In total, 236 were committed to D-Day along with 768 smaller Landing Craft Tank (LCT) and forty-eight Landing Craft Tank (Armoured). The LCTs could carry five Sherman DD (amphibious) tanks.

The naval element of Operation Overlord (D-Day) came under the designation of Operation Neptune. Implementing Neptune on 6 June 1944 required one of the largest seaborne invasion fleets in history, comprising: 1,213 warships, 4,126 landing ships and landing craft, and 1,600 other craft – almost 7,000 vessels in total.

Once all these craft had been assembled, the major challenge for the planners was the loading and landing schedule. General Francis de Guingand, Chief of Staff of General Bernard Montgomery's 21st Army Group recalled, 'Many of the ships carrying vehicles and equipment, although not required at once, had to be loaded before D-Day. Relative priorities so much depended upon the course of the campaign, and therefore decisions at this early date were not easy. For instance, by what date would another load of bridging be required? This depended, of course, upon our rate of progress. When would the 12th US Army Group take over? If we shipped over all their vehicles too soon, valuable space might be wasted. Such problems came up each day.'

On D-Day itself the Allies successfully landed 155,000 troops, 6,000 vehicles (including 900 tanks), 600 guns and about 4,000 tons of supplies. Quite remarkably, within five days 326,547 troops, 54,186 vehicles and 104,428 tons of supplies had been brought ashore. This momentum, though, was lost once the weather deteriorated and on 19 June a storm halted all crossings in the English Channel for three vital days.

The two Mulberry artificial harbours began to disintegrate: the one off Omaha Beach was written off and used to repair the British one at Arromanches. The build-up virtually ground to a halt, delaying 20,000 vehicles and 140,000 tons of stores; however, by the end of the month over 850,000 men, 148,000 vehicles, and 570,000 tons of supplies had been landed, taking the battle far into the Normandy countryside.

Just four LCTs were lost during Neptune and Landing Ship (Infantry) *Empire Broadsword* was sunk by a mine off Normandy on 2 July 1944. The LSTs continued to support operations and by the end of September they had brought 41,035 wounded men back across the English Channel as well as thousands of PoWs.

By the time of Operation Goodwood on 18 July 1944 the Allies' tank strength stood at almost 5,900 and continued to rise, reaching almost 6,760 a week later when Operation Cobra was launched. When the Germans commenced their Avranches–Mortain counter-attack in early August, the US Army could muster almost 4,000 tanks. Allied industrial muscle meant that losses were quickly replaced: for example, three British armoured divisions were able to shrug off the loss of 400 tanks following two days of heavy fighting during Goodwood; replacements arrived within thirty-six hours.

The most common Allied tank deployed in the battle for Normandy was the American Sherman M4 and M4A1 – these equipped the bulk of the American, British, Canadian, French and Polish armoured forces committed to the campaign. Note the extra plate armour welded to the hulls and turrets. (*US Army/NARA*)

At the time of D-Day up-gunned Shermans were in very short supply. Only 800 M4s armed with a 105mm gun were produced during 1943; one is seen here in Normandy in the first shot. The follow-on M4A3 (again with a 105mm gun) only went into production in April 1944. Likewise the M4A1 and M4A3 (seen here in this second shot), equipped with a 76mm gun, had only become available in early 1944. (*US Army/NARA*)

To try and compensate for the Sherman's lack of punch in June 1942 the Americans began to produce the M10, armed with a 3in gun using the Sherman chassis. In British service it was known as the Wolverine, and from late 1944 the gun was replaced with a British 17-pounder to create the Achilles. Likewise, the American M36, armed with a powerful 90mm gun, did not enter service in north-west Europe until late 1944. (*US Army/NARA*)

An M7 Priest 105mm self-propelled gun, belonging to the 66th Armored Field Artillery Battalion, US 4th Armored Division, en route to St Lô in Normandy. The M7 and M7B1 (which used the M3 and M4 medium tank chassis) were standard equipment for the artillery battalions in all American armoured divisions. They were also used to equip some of the artillery battalions with British armoured divisions during D-Day, but Sextons replaced these a few days after the landings. (US Army/NARA)

The American M5 light tank is easily distinguished from the earlier M3 by the stepped rear deck. From early 1943 the M5A1 replaced the M5 on the production line. In British service it was designated the Stuart VI and a small number were delivered during 1943–44. (US Army/NARA)

The M8 Howitzer Motor Carriage utilised the M5's chassis and was armed with a 75mm howitzer. This was used to equip the HQ companies of the US Army's medium tank battalions. The crew of this vehicle from the US 2nd Armored Division has dubbed it 'Laxative'. (*US Army/NARA*)

The most significant British-built tank in Normandy was the Cromwell, also armed with a 75mm gun. Along with the Sherman it formed the main equipment of the British armoured divisions. This particular example is negotiating a Normandy hedgerow. (*Author's Collection*)

The M8 was in fact the only armoured car to be employed in action by the US Army. It had an open-topped, circular cast turret armed with a 37mm gun and two machine guns. This was a six-wheeled vehicle and saw extensive service in north-west Europe. This vehicle's turret is reversed for reasons best known to the crew. (*US Army/NARA*)

British Churchill tanks
embarking *LST 239*
prior to D-Day.
Armed with a 75mm
gun like other British
tanks, by 1944–45 the
Churchill was under-
gunned by German
standards. These
examples appear to
have cast turrets and
are Churchill Mk IVs
(identifiable by the
square escape doors)
upgraded to Mk VII
standard with 75mm
guns. (*Author's
Collection*)

The British Sherman IIC, IVC and VC Firefly were the only Allied tanks capable of taking on the Panther or Tiger on equal terms (using the M4A1, M4A3 and M4A4 respectively). However, the Firefly was not given production priority until February 1944 and initially they were issued on the basis of one per troop due to the shortage of 17-pounder guns. The British Army should have been equipped with the new Challenger tank armed with the 17-pounder, but teething problems meant that it was not produced until March 1944 and no one had thought to make it waterproof – ruling out a role for it on D-Day. The Avenger self-propelled gun, also under development and armed with the same gun, did not appear until 1946. (*Author's Collection*)

A troop of Sextons, identifiable by their muzzle breaks, providing indirect fire. The Sexton was the British answer to the American M7 Howitzer Motor Carriage; it was built in Canada again, using the M3 and M4 bogies. This mounted the standard British 25-pounder field gun in place of the 105mm. The Sexton was used to replace the M7, which had entered British service in 1942, in the field regiments of the armoured divisions; a process completed by mid-1944 ready for D-Day. (*Author's Collection*)

Key to getting Allied armour ashore was the Landing Ship Tank, or LST, which could carry up to 60 vehicles, and the smaller Landing Craft Tank, or LCT. These craft could land armoured vehicles dry-shod, without the need for them to enter the water. (*US Navy/NARA*)

Amphibious warfare required specialist equipment and this US Navy LST and the DUKW amphibious truck were state of the art in 1944. (*US Navy/NARA*)

Among the vehicles stored on the upper deck of this LST are a number of 'soft-skinned' (i.e. unarmoured) vehicles belonging to the 346th Field Company, Royal Army Service Corps, attached to the 50th (Northumbrian) Infantry Division, which landed on Gold Beach on 6 June 1944. Note the white star aerial recognition symbol. (*US Army/NARA*)

The Allies planned, amidst great secrecy, to land their vehicles and other heavy equipment dry-shod via two enormous prefabricated harbours, codenamed 'Mulberries', off Gold and Omaha Beaches. Each beach was to be protected by an off-shore breakwater, or 'Gooseberry', created by old ships that would be sunk. Hollow ferro-concrete caissons would then fill any gaps in the blockship line. (*Author's Collection*)

Inside each Mulberry were three floating piers against which vessels could offload in relatively calm water. Floating roadways were bolted together to link the piers to the beaches. (*Author's Collection*)

This demonstrates one of the floating piers in use. The *LST 21* crewed by US coastguard personnel, has just unloaded 'Virgin', a Sherman belonging to the HQ of the 8th Independent Armoured Brigade at Gold Beach in June 1944. The Austin K5 to its left belongs to the Nottinghamshire Yeomanry (Sherwood Rangers), who were also attached to the 8th Armoured Brigade. (*Author's Collection*)

Another shot showing one of the American piers being used to offload trucks. (*US Navy/NARA*)

'Hurricane', a Sherman belonging to H Company, US 2nd Armored Division, disembarking from a LST probably on 8 or 9 June 1944. Note the deep-water wading gear. The air inlet and exhaust shrouds would have permitted the tank's engine to breath had it been forced to wade ashore. (*US Army/NARA*)

This row of fourteen Sherman tanks and their supporting infantry makes for an impressive sight. These American tankers are training for their role in north-west Europe at Camp McCain, Mississippi during 24 May–18 June 1944. The tanks belong to the US 5th Armoured Division and the GIs are from the 94th Infantry Division. (*Author's Collection*)

Chapter Three

Hobart's 'Funnies'

Having learned a very nasty lesson from the disastrous Dieppe raid in 1942 (where armour was unable to penetrate inland), the British military realised that it was vital to have specialised armoured fighting vehicles (AFVs) that could punch right through the hard crust of Hitler's Atlantic Wall defences. The Allied assault on his *Festung Europa*, or 'Fortress Europe', saw British military ingenuity at is best, resulting in a unique armoured division.

Major-General Sir Percy Hobart was first tasked with developing novel ways of assaulting *Festung Europa*, in April 1943. General Francis de Guingand, Chief of Staff of Montgomery's 21st Army Group, was delighted about 'Hobo' Hobart's appointment, for it was to be his drive and personality that was largely responsible for the success of the project. 'Some of the staff under me would become terrified when they knew General Hobo was about,' recalled de Guingand with amusement. 'He was such a go getter that they never really knew until he had left what new commitment they had been persuaded to accept.'

From its creation in 1942 the British 79th Armoured Division was a regular armoured unit, but the following year, with the impending invasion of Nazi-occupied France, it was earmarked for a specialised role. In fact its task was so secret that the existence of the division was not publicly acknowledged until after the Rhine crossing in March 1945. Even then specifications of some of the vehicles, such as the swimming DD tank, were withheld until September 1945.

Hobart's 79th became affectionately known as the 'Funnies' because of its unique armour. It became the largest division in the British Army and, by the time of the Rhine crossing, consisted of five brigades operating 1,916 specialised vehicles and gun tanks (compared to a normal armoured division's complement of 350 AFVs) and 4,762 soft-skin vehicles. While it never fought together as a whole division, it has the distinction of being the only armoured formation to have units fight with every brigade, division and corps of the British and Canadian armies in north-west Europe from June 1944 onwards.

Initially Hobart's 'Funnies' were equipped with just three principal types of specialised armour. The most immediate problem facing the Allies was to get their armour ashore as quickly as possible to support the assault infantry – landing craft were vulnerable and the larger landing ships could only offload once the beaches had been made secure. The solution was the amphibious Sherman Duplex Drive (DD) or 'swimming' tank. Three regiments of the 79th were equipped with this: the 4th/7th Royal Dragoon Guards, the 13th/18th Hussars and the 1st East Riding Yeomanry.

The DD tank was designed by Nicholas Straussler, who found waterproofing the vehicle's hull and raising the freeboard could make a tank float without cumbersome buoyancy aids. This was done by erecting a canvas screen round the hull; initial success in 1943–44 was achieved with the conversion of Valentine tanks, a few of which saw service in Italy. The crews were not keen on the newer Sherman, as they were larger and heavier than the Valentines. Although the freeboard was higher on the Sherman this did not prevent it shipping alarming amounts of water in choppy seas.

The Sherman DD tank consisted of steel decking around the hull, upon which a screen could be raised by thirty-six air tubes and secured by hinged struts. Importantly the front screen could be lowered to facilitate firing. The Duplex Drive – propellers and tracks – could manage a slow 4–5 knots, and although the low silhouette in the water enabled an element of tactical surprise on D-Day they had a nasty habit of capsizing in rough water.

Once ashore, specialised vehicles, known as the Churchill AVREs (Armoured Vehicle Royal Engineers) – consisting of various equipment mounted on Churchill tank chassis – were designed to deal with the Germans' concrete sea defences. Churchill Mk III and IV tanks were equipped with a massive 290mm Petard spigot mortar for 'bunker busting'. Some of these, nicknamed the 'Bobbin', were fitted with a carpet layer for crossing soft clay and sand. Other variants included the ARK (Armoured Ramp Carrier), the mine-clearing Bullshorn Plough (which was only used on the Normandy beaches) and the SBG (Small Box Girder) Assault Bridge. All these vehicles were operated by the 5th and 6th Assault Regiments Royal Engineers (ARE).

The third specialised AFV was the Sherman Crab, designed to clear defended minefields and barbed wire. It consisted of a British Sherman V (M4A4) gun tank fitted with a rotating flail, driven by the main drive shaft, with an effective depth of about five inches. Three regiments of the 79th were equipped with Crabs: the 22nd Dragoons, 1st Lothian and Border Yeomanry and the Westminster Dragoons.

In the DD tank regiments the 3-ton lorries were replaced with the amphibious 6x6 DUKW, which were veterans of the campaigns in the Mediterranean. The prototype was built around the cab of a six-wheel-drive GMC military truck, with the addition of a watertight hull and a propeller. However, it was not an armoured vehicle and, at 7.5 tons, managed a top speed of just 6.4mph in water or a respectable 55mph on land. The DUKW rode the waves well and its bilge pumps meant it could be kept free of water and was ideal for ferrying stores from ship to shore. Less glamorously the division was also equipped with armoured bulldozers: mainly the American Caterpillar Tractor Company's D.8, protected by an armoured superstructure and engine cover.

As well as punching through the sea defences Hobart's forces were also tasked with helping to deal with the various man-made obstacles that obstructed the shoreline. The best methods devised were to blow them up with demolition charges or simply drag them out of the way. 'I paid a visit to see these activities,' said General de Guingand, 'and returned feeling that yet another "horror" had been laid low.'

In the run up to the landings, replicas of German coastal defences were built at the Orford training area in Suffolk, where the various vehicles were put through their paces and techniques refined. DD tank swimming training was undertaken at Osborne Bay, the Isle of Wight, Stokes Bay, Gosport and Studland Bay, Dorset, amongst other places.

Some 30,000 DD launches were made during the exercises and officially there was just one death. Nonetheless, rumour amongst the tank crews was that the 4th/7th Dragoon Guards lost six tanks with six fatalities off Poole. 'On one occasion,' recalled Lieutenant Stuart Hills of the Sherwood Rangers Yeomanry, 'I received orders from the squadron leader by radio to launch in conditions I deemed suicidal.' Luckily good sense prevailed.

The first formal rehearsals involving the 'Funnies' were conducted at Studland in front of a very high-ranking audience, including the king, General Bernard Montgomery and the Allied Supreme Commander General Dwight Eisenhower. De Guingand recalled, 'It was agreed at this conference that the DD tanks would be the first to land, and that the self-propelled artillery would be positioned in the rear, firing over the leading waves. Naval ships would support the assault from the flanks. No fixed rule was made for the different gun devices [i.e. the Funnies]. A "menu" would be selected to suit the problem presented by the particular beach in question. This arrangement worked very well.'

By the summer of 1944, after a great deal of hard training and assimilation of this new kit, the division consisted of four brigades: 27th Armoured (DDs), 30th Armoured (Crabs), 1st Assault Royal Engineers (AVREs) and 1st Tank (CDL – Canal Defence Light, which was not used during D-Day). The Americans declined the offer of such vehicles, except for the DD tanks, and this was to have ramifications for the American troops assaulting Omaha Beach.

Allied planners quickly realised that specialised armoured support was vital in helping the assaulting infantry overcome German strongpoints such as this gun position. Hitler's coastal defences that formed *Festung Europa* comprised concrete bunkers, emplaced field and anti-tank guns protected by concrete pillboxes and extensive minefields and barbed wire. It was this hard 'crust' that the Allies' assault forces had to break through. (*Author's Collection*)

One of the biggest threats, apart from mines, to Allied armour coming ashore were heavily emplaced German anti-tank guns such as this one – now under 'new management' following the landings. This appears to be an 88mm PaK 43/41, which was the cheap and cheerful version of the early PaK 43. (*Author's Collection*)

A key worry for Allied planners was that emplaced enemy guns would knock out the LSTs and LCTs before they ever reached the shore. (*US Army/NARA*)

German coastal defences also included emplaced tank turrets armed with anti-tank guns. In this case an early model Panzer Mk IV turret with the short 75mm gun has been given a second career. (*US Army/NARA*)

Another threat to landing craft were mines attached to poles sitting just below the water line. On D-Day tanks were able to swim over or around many such obstacles. (*US Army/NARA*)

A Sherman DD (Duplex Drive) tank with its floatation screen partially raised. The crews found these swimming tanks dangerous, as they could not cope with choppy seas. The most immediate problem for the Allies was to get their tanks ashore quickly to support the assaulting infantry, and the simple solution was the swimming tank. (*Author's Collection*)

Once ashore the Churchill AVRE (converted from a Churchill Mk IV), sporting the massive 290mm Petard spigot mortar – known as the 'flying dustbin' – had the job of 'bunker busting'. Little could withstand such a blast. The second image shows the tank using a fascine to cross an anti-tank ditch. (*Author's Collection*)

The third specialised armoured fighting vehicle was the Sherman Crab, seen here kicking up the dust with its flail in the first two shots. Designed to clear minefields and barbed wire, it consisted of the M4A4 fitted with a rotating flail. These successfully helped clear mines on the invasion beaches and beyond. Three regiments were equipped with these tanks and fifty were deployed on Gold, Juno and Sword Beaches. (*Author's Collection*)

The 79th Armoured Division also employed the American D.8 bulldozer fitted with an armoured superstructure. These carried out various tasks on the beaches and the beachhead, clearing obstacles, filling craters and creating ramps. However, the thin armour only afforded protection from rifle and machine-gun fire, and, as the tracks were flimsy, mines easily disabled them. These American D.8s at work on one of the American beaches, and later in the bridgehead, lack the armoured superstructure and engine covers. In the second shot an American bulldozer clears the smashed remains of two Panzer Lehr Panzer Mk IVs from the road on 27 July 1944. Judging by the extreme damage to the tank in the foreground they were caught in an air attack. (*US Army/NARA*)

A Royal Marines' Centaur IV armed with a 95mm howitzer. These tanks also had a bunker-busting role, but many were knocked out on the beaches. About 950 Centaur Cruiser tanks (forerunner of the Cromwell) were built, of which 80 were close-support models with a 95mm howitzer replacing the standard 6-pounder gun. The latter were assigned to the Royal Marines Armoured Support Group and saw action on D-Day providing covering fire from LCTs and then on the beaches. Some Centaur IIIs were later converted to a 'dozer role with the removal of the turret and the addition of a 'dozer blade. (*Author's Collection*)

In the DD tank regiments the 3-tonners were replaced with DUKWs. The DUKW rode the waves well and its bilge pumps meant it could be kept free of water – it was ideal for ferrying stores from ship to shore. More than 21,000 DUKWs were manufactured, with large numbers supplied to the British Army. (*Author's Collection*)

An American DUKW is manoeuvred into *LST 543* prior to D-Day. The prototype amphibious six-wheel-drive DUKW was built around the cab of a GMC military truck, with the addition of a watertight hull and a propeller. It was not an armoured vehicle and at 7.5 tons managed a top speed of just 6.4mph in water, with a more respectable 55mph on land. (*US Navy/NARA*)

Once the beachhead was secure, the larger landing craft were able to land their vehicles dry-shod. (*Author's Collection*)

The fact that the Americans did not take up the offer of specialised armour, apart from DD tanks, was certainly a contributing factor in the heavy casualties they suffered on Omaha Beach. (*US Army/NARA*)

Most of the American Shermans were landed dry-shod on D-Day due to the stormy weather. (*US Army/NARA*)

While the Churchill AVRE was ideal for dealing with German bunkers, many still proved all but impregnable. This one had received in excess of fifteen direct hits and survived. (*US Army/NARA*)

Having cleared the beaches, Canadian infantry shelter behind a Sherman tank advancing through a French village. DD tanks acted as the vanguard for the Canadian 7th and 8th Brigades on Juno Beach. (*Canadian Army/Canadian National Archives*)

An AVRE hidden by its vast bundle of fascines, which were used for crossing tank traps. The Assault Engineers deployed 120 on D-Day, losing twenty-two of them during the process of getting off the beaches. (*Author's Collection*)

Chapter Four

Failure at Bayeux and Caen

Due to varying tide times and durations of supporting bombardment, the landings on the invasion beaches, stretching from La Madeleine in the west to Ouistreham in the east, were staggered. The American Utah and Omaha Beaches were assaulted at 0630 hours on 6 June 1944, while the British Gold and Sword Beach assaults were at 0725 hours and the Canadian Juno Beach at 0745 hours.

Utah, forming the far western flank, centred roughly on La Madeleine, was assaulted by Major-General J. Lawton Collins, US 7th Corps, led by the US 4th Infantry Division. Their job was to link up with the US 82nd and 101st Airborne Divisions, establishing a bridgehead over the River Vire and the nearby canal ready to link up with Omaha to the east.

Due to the tide the American GIs went ashore 1,000 yards south of their planned landing zone. Twenty-nine Sherman DD tanks spearheaded the assault and were launched 5,000 yards from the shore. Little resistance was encountered – consisting mainly of small-arms fire. Around 0800 hours Pouppeville was attacked, and the US 4th Infantry managed to push four miles inland, brushing aside most of the German resistance. By the end of the day the Americans had successfully put ashore 23,000 men, 1,700 vehicles and 1,700 tons of stores.

Major-General Leonard T. Gerow's US 5th Corps, led by the US 1st Infantry Division, attacked Omaha Beach, which was bordered by Vierville-sur-Mer and Ste-Honorine. The preliminary bombardment lasted only forty minutes and consequently many of the German defences remained intact. The shingle beach was also bordered by marshland and a high bluff, making it an ideal fire zone.

Thanks to the rough seas and enemy fire, only five out of thirty-two DD tanks cleared Omaha Beach, while out of the fifty-one tanks landed dry-shod by the assault craft eight were knocked out before even clearing the beach. Under heavy machine-gun, mortar and artillery fire the GIs were cut to pieces as they staggered from the water, and without armoured support they were unable to clear the beach quickly.

The Americans had declined the offer of British 'Funnies', and German fire was so intense that only two of the engineers' sixteen bulldozers put ashore on the right side of the beach remained serviceable. By 0900 a few Americans had reached the top of the bluff and were beginning to move inland towards the villages. However, the GIs suffered an appalling 2,500 casualties and only managed to get two miles inland, though by nightfall 33,000 men were ready for the subsequent offensive.

The British and Canadian eastern task force attacked a broad twenty-five-mile front, between Port-en-Bessin and Ouistreham. Gold Beach, centred on Le Hamel and La Rivière, was assaulted by Lieutenant-General G.C. Bucknall's British 30th Corps, led by the 50th Infantry Division. Their task was to take Port-en-Bessin in order to link up with Gerow's US 5th Corps, thrust for St Leger on the Caen–Bayeux road and seize Bayeux.

At 0725 assault units of the 79th Armoured Division, consisting of Sherman Crabs and Churchill AVREs, went in. Once again, due to the rough sea the DD tanks could not be deployed in the water and had to be landed dry-shod; adding to their problems, the tide also rose thirty minutes early. The AVREs were late and Le Hamel proved to be heavily defended – the sanatorium had been converted into a German strongpoint and German artillery was sweeping the beach. Nevertheless by the afternoon Port-en-Bessin had been taken.

By 2100 hours Arromanches had fallen, but the drive on Bayeux had stalled, even though the Germans had largely abandoned it. The route west from Caen had also been captured, but at the end of the day a six-mile gap existed between the troops from Gold and Omaha Beaches. About 25,000 men had been put ashore and 50th Division had punched six miles inland.

At Juno the assaulting formation was the Canadian 3rd Infantry Division under Lieutenant-General J.T. Crocker's British 1st Corps. The beach was centred on Courseulles and Bernieres. The Canadians were to seize the two towns and drive their tanks flat out for Carpiquet airfield, west of Caen. In order to ensure the sea carried their landing craft over the reefs, the assault was timed for 0745, but because of the rough water they were delayed until 0800 hours. While landing craft did get over the reefs and most of the beach obstacles, their return trips were disastrous.

Only twenty-nine DD tanks were launched, with twenty-one of them reaching the shore – the rest had to be landed dry-shod from the landing craft. The 1st Hussars Regiment, B Squadron, supporting the Regina Rifles, landed at Courseulles at 0755 hours with fourteen (out of nineteen) tanks. Seven A Squadron tanks landed a few minutes after the Winnipeg Rifles on the beach west of Courseulles. Five more tanks were then landed by a LCT which had had earlier problems with its ramp.

Arriving before their armour the Canadian infantry found many of the German positions intact. As they were under heavy small-arms fire, they could not get off the beach and many of them were mown down trying to reach the shelter of a sea defence wall at the rear of the beach. Lacking armour support the Canadian infantry faltered, but an AVRE managed to blow a hole in the twelve-foot-high sea-wall, and they began to move inland. By the end of the day 21,500 men had been landed, and had made contact with the British 50th Division at La Rivière.

Crocker's 1st Corps, led by the British 3rd Infantry Division, assaulted Sword Beach, centred on Lion-sur-Mer. Their key objective was to take the city of Caen, the Germans' regional HQ, and link up with the airborne bridgehead over the River Orne to the east. H-Hour was 0725 and the spearhead DD tanks were launched 5,000 yards from the shore; out of thirty-four successfully launched only three were lost. By the evening 29,000 men were ashore in the Sword area.

While 21st Panzer Division moved to secure the Caen area during the night of 7 June the British 50th Infantry Division took Bayeux. The following day the US 1st Infantry Division captured Tour-en-Bessin and Le Coudrai on the Bayeux–Isigny road. Fortunately for the Allies the powerful Panzer Lehr Division was unable to attack towards Bayeux until the 9th. Running into Bucknall's 30th Corps it suffered heavy losses and only got to within three miles of the city before having to change to the defensive role.

This forced the British to shift their efforts west of Caen to the flank of Panzer Lehr and the high ground beyond Villers-Bocage. The idea of a right hook was Major-General G.W. Erskine's, commander of the 7th Armoured Division, and it was hoped that the move would break up the resistance in front of the 50th (Northumbrian) Division; it was also hoped to encircle the troublesome Panzer Lehr and break the logjam around Caen.

British tank crews in southern England preparing for D-Day, taking an inventory of their stores. This column of Churchill Mk IVs is believed to be at Stokes Bay, Gosport getting ready for embarkation at Portsmouth. (*Author's Collection*)

An American M10 tank destroyer by the name of 'Bessie' leads a column of vehicles out of an LST. This photo was taken during a training exercise at Slapton Sands, England prior to Operation Overlord. (*US Army/NARA*)

Operation Overlord begins. British Airspeed AS 51 Horsa gliders; the Horsa flew under both British and American colours during the Normandy invasion. In the early hours of 6 June three airborne divisions were parachuted and inserted by glider on either flank of the five invasion beaches to forestall counter-attacks. In particular the British 6th Airborne Division landed within striking distance of the 21st Panzer Division. The paras took with them a handful of glider-borne Tetrarch light tanks – these only saw service for a few days. (US Army/NARA)

These Martin B-26 Marauder bombers are softening up targets on D-Day – note their striped recognition markings. Allied medium and fighter-bombers did all they could to prevent the panzers reaching the beachhead. (USAAF/NARA)

Due to the differing tide times on 6 June 1944 the landings on the five invasion beaches were staggered. First, though, intensive naval and aerial bombardment were carried out in an effort to silence the German defences. (US Navy/NARA)

A dramatic aerial photo clearly showing the LSTs disgorging their vehicles onto one of the invasion beaches. (*Author's Collection*)

This photograph, probably taken on 8 or 9 June 1944 during the arrival of the US 2nd Armored Division, shows the incredible scene on Omaha Beach in front of Colleville-sur-Mer as LSTs beach directly onto the sand to allow their cargoes to disembark. (*US Army/NARA*)

This American half-track being landed dry-shod appears to be fitted with an anti-aircraft gun – though the Luftwaffe did very little to oppose the Normandy landings. (*US Army/NARA*)

After the Mulberry harbours had been created to form breakwaters, the LCTs were able to land their cargoes directly onto the floating piers. (*US Navy/NARA*)

Once the LSTs had ferried their tanks and soft-skinned vehicles across the English Channel they were then used to ferry German PoWs back to Britain and captivity. These US Military Police with fixed bayonets are clearly taking no chances, though the prisoners hardly look like the cream of the German Army. (*US Signal Corps/NARA*)

Pushing inland, Allied armour did not have it all its own way, as these burnt out Shermans testify. (*Author's Collection*)

A column of Shermans and M10 tank destroyers pass though a shattered Norman town. While the Americans drove on Cherbourg, the failure of British and Canadian forces to secure the city of Caen in the opening days of the invasion was to prove a major problem. (*US Army/NARA*)

Although Canadian armour had pushed through to Carpiquet airfield by 8 June 1944, the 12th SS Hitlerjugend Panzer Division stopped them dead in their tracks, destroying a total of twenty-seven tanks for the loss of fourteen panzers. The 12th SS held onto the airfield until early July. (*Canadian Army/Canadian National Archives*)

A King Tiger of Tiger II lays concealed at the road side in a desperate bid to avoid Allied fighter-bombers. Many German panzers ended up looking like mobile bushes as they struggled to move north to counter Operation Overlord. (*Author's Collection*)

A British Sherman Firefly pauses amidst a cornfield, its commander ever vigilant for any sign of counter-attacking panzers. (*Author's Collection*)

Two Sherman Armored Recovery Vehicles attend a disabled Sherman that has shed its tracks. It is from the 32nd Tank Regiment, Combat Command B, US 3rd Armored Division. By this stage in the war Allied tank recovery capabilities had greatly improved following hard-won lessons in North Africa. (*US Army/NARA*)

British Shermans pushing inland against the 12th SS Panzer Division. (*Author's Collection*)

An American M7 self-propelled gun takes shelter beneath some trees near a German grave. Following the invasion the US Army fought a largely infantry-based battle as it moved to liberate the Cotentin peninsula and Cherbourg. In contrast, to the east the British and Canadian Armies found themselves fighting a series of brutal tank battles against the gathering panzer divisions. (*US Signal Corps/NARA*)

Chapter Five

Off to the Races – Operation Epsom

Of all the setbacks that the Allies suffered during the Normandy campaign, the failure of Operation Perch on 13 June 1944 ranks as one of the worst. Just a week after D-Day, in the space of five minutes, a handful of Tigers destroyed the spearhead of 7th Armoured Division, saved the Panzer Lehr Division from encirclement, prevented the German line from being rolled up and stopped the Allies from breaking out to the south-west of Caen. In short, this engagement could have speeded the conclusion of the Normandy campaign, but instead poor planning and bad luck resulted in a major setback.

After D-Day both the Allies and the Germans knew that the strategic ground lay to the east, where the British 2nd Army was fighting around the city of Caen. Just to the south-east lay open tank country that could facilitate the Allies' breakout. After the Germans had successfully blunted General Montgomery's initial advances, he decided that, rather than fight a bloody frontal battle for Caen, 2nd Army would launch its main effort to the west towards Villers-Bocage and Evrecy, and then south-east towards Falaise.

Montgomery committed his two veteran divisions, the 51st Highland and 7th Armoured (the 'Desert Rats'), for two main flank attacks. The 51st were to attack through the British 6th Airborne Division, east of the Orne, and the 7th Armoured would attack to the south-west. The 51st's attack on 11 June was crushed and two days later their assault had petered out. The 7th Armoured's advance was slow, but a hole in the German line between Villers-Bocage and Caumont was detected. Greeted by joyful locals, the advance elements of Major-General G.W. Erskine's 7th Armoured entered Villers-Bocage on 13 June.

Unbeknown to the British a Tiger tank company under Lieutenant Michael Wittmann had occupied Point 213, dominating the road to Caen just north-east of Villers-Bocage. The British were outclassed from the start. The Cromwell, which had replaced 7th Armoured's Sherman tanks when they left Italy, was insufficiently armoured or armed. In stark contrast, the crew of a Tiger tank could expect to remain unharmed by the majority of Allied tanks except at point-blank range.

The distance between the British tanks and the supporting infantry proved too great a gap, allowing the German infantry to hold up the armour. The 4th County of London Yeomanry, known as the 'Sharpshooters', was over confident, with poor tank–infantry cooperation and inadequate dispersion. While the Tiger was a vastly superior tank to the light Cromwell, this was still no excuse for the damage that Wittman inflicted at Villers-Bocage. In short it was an intelligence disaster.

Wittmann's prompt action in thwarting the British enabled Villers-Bocage to be retaken later in the day (by Panzer Lehr and units of the 2nd Panzer battle group), thus plugging the gap. In total 7th Armoured lost 225 men, twenty-seven tanks, fourteen half-tracks, fourteen Bren carriers and a number of anti-tank guns. The only consolation for the British was that by 18/19 June Panzer Lehr had lost about 100 of its 260 tanks in the fighting in the Villers-Bocage area. Its commander, General Fritz Bayerlein, claimed that this weakened his division so much that it was incapable of launching an armoured thrust towards the sea. By 1 August Panzer Lehr had just twenty-seven tanks.

Wittmann's successful defensive action forced Montgomery to launch two more costly enveloping attacks – Operation Epsom to the west of Caen on 25 June and Operation Goodwood to the east on 18 July. It seemed that thanks to the overwhelming number of British tanks Epsom could not fail, but directly in its path lay the 12th SS Panzer Division (supported by the 2nd Heavy Tank Company with Tiger tanks). Bucknall's 30th Corps was to attack first, followed by Lieutenant-General Sir Riard O'Connor's 8th Corps. The latter had 60,000 men, 600 tanks, 300 guns and the support of another 400 guns from 30th Corps, as well as naval and air support.

The plan was for 8th Corps to break through the German lines, between the 47th Panzer Corps and 1st SS Panzer Corps, force a bridgehead over the Odon River and take the strategic height of Hill 112. For the British it was a race against time as the 2nd Panzer Corps and 2nd SS Panzer Division were heading for the sector; even if the attack pierced the deep defences of the 12th SS the intervention of German armoured reinforcements could kill Epsom.

On 25 June 30th Corps conducted Operation Dauntless – a subsidiary attack that secured 8th Corps' western flank before the main offensive, which was to be carried out by the 49th (West Riding) Infantry Division, supported by the 8th Armoured Brigade. The 49th also conducted Operation Martlet intended to capture Fontenay-le-Pesnil.

By 30 June 30th Corps had fought its way to Rauray and Tessel, but in the face of determined resistance from 2nd SS it could not maintain its momentum and failed to reach the Odon. In contrast, 8th Corps forced its way over the river, creating a narrow bridgehead between Gavrus to the west and Baron to the east. Although the Epsom offensive towards Evrecy, south of Caen, was a tactical failure, the Orne was crossed, Hill 112 was taken and a deep salient was driven into the German defences west of Caen.

The 2nd SS Panzer Corps was ordered to strike the corridor, created by the 15th (Scottish) Division, from the south-west. The 9th SS Panzer Division was to attack towards le Valtru and the Cheux bottleneck, supported by 2nd SS and Panzer Lehr, while the 10th SS would assault the Odon bridgehead and Hill 112. Elements of the 1st SS, 12th SS and 21st Panzer divisions were also to be involved in attacking the other flank of the exposed corridor.

In countering Epsom the panzers of the 10th SS attacked the Gavrus bridgehead on the flank of Major-General G.P.B. Roberts' 11th Armoured Division on Hill 112. The usual problem – shortage of fuel – greatly limited the number of panzers that the division could initially throw at Roberts. Nonetheless, the 12th SS attacked Hill 112 from the east and by midday on the 30th were on the summit.

Epsom cost the British 8th Corps 4,020 casualties; the 11th Armoured Division alone lost 100 tanks and suffered 1,000 casualties during 26–29 June. While the Germans succeeded in containing Epsom, it was at a cost: 12th SS had lost over 2,600 casualties, while 9th SS suffered 1,145 casualties and lost sixteen Panzer IVs, six Panthers and ten StuG IIIs.

A knocked-out Sturmgeschütz 40 from the 17th SS Panzergrenadier Division, Götz von Berlichingen. During their counter-attack on 13 June at Carentan they got to within 500 yards of the town before they were driven off by units from the US 2nd Armored and US 101st Airborne Divisions. That same day the British 7th Armoured Division suffered a major setback to the east at Villers-Bocage. (*US Army/NARA*)

Another abandoned StuG. This type of assault gun was ideally suited for German defensive operations in the Normandy countryside. Independent German armoured forces (i.e. not belonging to the panzer or infantry divisions) included five Sturmgeschütz units. (*Author's Collection*)

GIs and curious French sightseers clamber over a Tiger I. The Germans had two SS heavy tank battalions, the 101st and 102nd, available in Normandy. The 101st in early June had thirty-seven Tigers on its strength. While this unit was famous in its own right, famed tank ace Michael Wittmann commanded the 2nd company. (*US Army/NARA*)

Members of the 51st Highland Division questioning German PoWs, who in this instance are foreign 'volunteers'. These men are members of the Turkestan Legion that provided twenty-six combat battalions and included Kazakhs, Kirghiz, Uzbeks, Turkomans and Karakalpaks, some of whom ended up in France. (*Author's Collection*)

An abandoned Sharpshooters' Cromwell tank in Villers-Bocage following the engagement on 13 June 1944 which stopped Operation Perch west of Caen. The Cromwell, which replaced the 7th Armoured Division's Shermans when they redeployed from Italy, was simply too lightly armoured to stand up to the firepower of the Tiger. (*Author's Collection*)

Another victim of the Tigers, this time a Sharpshooters' Sherman – note how the round penetrated the turret on the left-hand side. It was only when the Tigers attacked for a second time at Villers-Bocage that the British were able to get the better of them. (*Author's Collection*)

Wittmann's Tiger lies disabled amidst the rubble of a subsequent Allied bombing raid on Villers-Bocage. Behind it lay another Tiger and a Panzer Mk IV. While he and his crew managed to escape unharmed, clearly his tank did not after running into a British trap. By this stage, however, it did not matter, as he had already blunted 7th Armoured Division's thrust and German reinforcements were en route. (*Author's Collection*)

In the late afternoon RAF Typhoons were called in to help cover the British withdrawal from Villers-Bocage. However, while the Typhoons strafed and rocketed the main street, in reality they were probably attacking panzers that had already been knocked out following Wittmann's second foray into the town. (*Alan Jones Collection*)

Following Villers-Bocage, Montgomery launched two unsuccessful attacks to the west and east of Caen. During Operation Espom, launched on 25 June to the west, the British came up against teenage Nazis such as these young men who had been recruited into the 9th SS, 10th SS and 12th SS Panzer Divisions. (*US Army/NARA*)

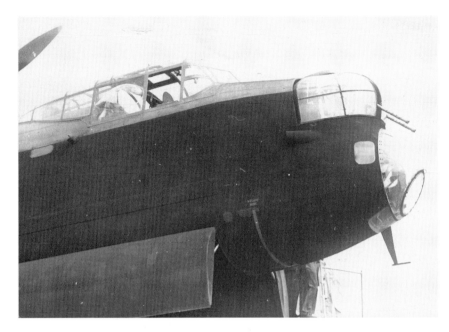

The business end of the RAF's Avro Lancaster bomber and in the second shot a Handley Page Halifax is taking on its bomb load. On 30 June the 'heavies' played their part when RAF Bomber Command learned that the 2nd and 9th Panzer Divisions were approaching Villers-Bocage. (*Author's Collection*)

On 30 June 1944 the RAF attacked Villers-Bocage in daylight with 250 bombers from Nos. 3 (Lancaster), 4 (Halifax) and 8 (Mosquito) Groups, supported by eight squadrons of Spitfires. They dropped 1,176 tons of bombs with devastating effects on the town and surrounding area. The Tiger in the distance is Wittmann's and nearby is the remains of a Panzer Mk IV, which seems to have been blown all the way down the street. (*Author's Collection*)

Epsom was intended as a pre-emptive attack to tie up German armour reinforcements. Eight derelict Sd Kfz 251/1 that belonged to panzergrenadiers of one of the panzer divisions can be seen: their positioning indicates they were probably abandoned. The 37mm flak gun in the centre, which appears to be a Sd Kfz 7/1 or Sd Kfz 6/2, clearly did them no good. (*Author's Collection*)

This derelict Tiger, which has shed its tracks, seems to have suffered a rather unusual fate, in that it has been incorporated into a log pile. (*Author's Collection*)

British infantry pose by captured German Goliaths – these packed a nasty punch if they reached their targets. There were at least two German remote control units in Normandy supporting the panzers. (*Author's Collection*)

While the British were struggling around Caen the Americans were securing the towns and villages to the west. This mobile hedgerow is concealing an American M10; to the right is a burnt-out Sherman, while on the left is the mangled remains of a German prime mover, behind which is an 88mm anti-tank gun. The German crewman running back up the road was probably killed by the direct hit on the half-track. (*US Army/NARA*)

Liberation is in the air. GIs examine a recently liberated French town, while an M8 armoured car stands guard. At moments like this enemy snipers were always a danger. (*US Army/NARA*)

The main German self-propelled anti-tank weapon in Normandy was the Marder, armed with the 75mm PaK 40/3. This particular example lies smashed after an encounter with the US Army. (*US Army/NARA*)

Chapter Six

Operation Charnwood

Immediately after D-Day tanks from the US 2nd, 3rd and 4th Armored Divisions pushed west, with 2nd Armored linking up with the 101st Airborne near the city of Carentan. Thrown into combat on 10 June 1944, the reconnaissance battalion of the 17th SS Panzergrenadier Division set about the American paratroops. Dubbed the Battle of Bloody Gulch, the paratroops were only saved by the timely arrival of the US 2nd Armored's tanks.

The presence of the 17th SS in the Carentan area helped persuade the Americans that they should first clear the Cotentin peninsula and capture the vital port of Cherbourg before making further efforts to strike southwards. While Montgomery's forces were struggling west of Caen, Major-General Collins' US 7th Corps fought its way up the Cotentin peninsula to Cherbourg and attacked the city on 22 June. After four days of fierce fighting, the garrison – some 21,000 men – surrendered.

By 1 July the Cotentin had been cleared, with US forces having entered Auderville on the Cap de la Hague, to the west of Cherbourg, and Barfleur to the east. Thanks to German demolition efforts, however, the port was not serviceable until mid-August. In the meantime, to the south a German defensive line took shape between Lessay and St Lô, which was held by the German 7th Army anchored around two panzer divisions and a panzergrenadier division.

The panzers in Normandy found it increasingly difficult to escape the attention of the Allied air forces, especially the bombers. Air Marshal Arthur Harris, in charge of RAF Bomber Command, recalled, 'On June 30th it was learned that the 2nd and 9th Panzer Divisions were moving up through Villers-Bocage to make an attack that night; there was a network of roads here which it would be almost impossible for the enemy to bypass and it was therefore the obvious place in which to bomb the panzer divisions and their equipment – the enemy had also established a supply point there. This time Bomber Command attacked in daylight and dropped 1,100 tons of bombs; the panzer divisions had to call off the planned attack.'

By the second week of July German divisions from the 15th Army in the Calais area were arriving in strength in Normandy. In order to keep them tied up in the

Caen sector and to prevent them gaining any sort of initiative that could dislodge the British and Canadians, the British 2nd Army struck northern Caen. On 7 July bombers flattened an area 4,000 yards long by 1,500 yards deep with 2,560 tons of bombs prior to the assault.

Then at 0420 hours the following day three divisions from the British 1st and Canadian 2nd Corps thrust into Caen with Operation Charnwood, the British frontal assault on the northern outskirts. The British attack had opened by carpet-bombing the city and a regiment from the 16th Luftwaffe Field Division all but vanished under the deluge. Within two days the Germans had been driven from Caen north of the Orne, but they tenaciously held on in the south and south-east thanks to the efforts of the Waffen-SS.

For three days elements of 1st SS Panzer Division fought alongside the 12th SS Panzer to the south-west of Caen to halt Charnwood. They found themselves up against Major-General R.F.L. Keller's Canadian 3rd Division, which struck towards the Odon. The British tried to force the panzers out of the way westwards with Operation Jupiter and Operation Greenline. From 10–15 July they launched a series of attacks, both west and east of the city, in order to keep the panzers tied down and to try and secure Caen. By 15 July the number of panzers in the American sector had risen to 190, while the number facing the British and Canadians was about 645.

Following the blunting of Charnwood, General von Obstfelder's 86th Corps, which included 21st Panzer, assumed 1st SS Panzer Corps' responsibility for the whole sector east of Caen. The 1st SS Panzer Division then assumed responsibility for the sector, taking over from the exhausted 12th SS. On the 15th the British launched Greenline, holding the 2nd, 9th SS and 10th SS Panzer Divisions west of Caen, along the Espom Salient, and obliging 1st SS to return to the fight to hold the Orne.

These diversionary operations meant that Montgomery, with the knowledge that the panzers were pinned down to the west, was poised to strike east of Caen three days later. By mid-July the Germans had suffered 97,000 casualties, and only 6,000 of the available 10,000 replacements had reached the front by that stage. Panzer losses totalled 225, with just seventeen replacements.

In the meantime, the US 7th, 8th and 19th Corps strove to reach their start line ready for the actual breakout, which was codenamed Operation Cobra. On 17 July they took St Lô and reached the St Lô–Periers road – having advanced only seven miles in seventeen days at the cost of 40,000 casualties. The breakout could not be launched before 20 July because of the required build up of supplies. The plan was to sweep south-east through Avranches and Mortain, thereby cutting off the panzers in Normandy.

It took the Americans two weeks to secure the Cotentin peninsula and the port of Cherbourg. The latter was captured along with 21,000 German troops, some of whom can be seen here marching into captivity. On D-Day one of the few armoured units in the area was Panzer Battalion 206, equipped with twenty-four second-hand French tanks at Cap de la Hague, the northernmost tip of the peninsula. It was swiftly wiped out in the fighting that followed. (*US Army/NARA*)

Below: While British armour such as this Cromwell and Sherman Firefly were slogging it out with the Germans either side of Caen, Montgomery decided to use three infantry divisions to seize the city west of the Orne River. The removal of the enemy salient west of the Orne meant that Monty could then extend the Allied bridgehead east of the river held by the hard-pressed 6th Airborne and 51st Highland Divisions. (*Author's Collection*)

On 7 July 1944 Allied bombers attacked the city of Caen as a prelude to Operation Charnwood. The target area on the northern outskirts was 4,000 yards wide and 1,500 yards deep which was hit by 460 aircraft between 2150 and 2230. (*Author's Collection*)

Great swathes of Caen were left flattened after the attentions of RAF Bomber Command and some German defenders were still stunned hours after the attack. However, while these attacks helped silence German resistance, they also rendered areas of the city impassable to Allied tanks. (*Author's Collection*)

RAF Typhoon fighter-bombers also provided close air support around Caen with pilots pressing home attacks on enemy armoured units. The intensity of German flak around the city resulted in heavy losses in both aircraft and pilots. The Normandy campaign was the heyday of the Typhoon and along with the USAAF's Mustang and Thunderbolt the Germans quickly learned to fear the Allied fighter-bombers. (*Alan Jones Collection*)

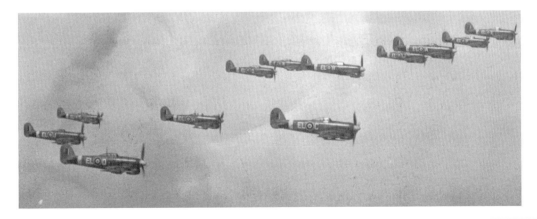

A Canadian tank column prepares for action; these men are believed to belong to the Canadian 4th Armoured Division. The Canadian 3rd Infantry Division found itself engaged in tough fighting with units of the Waffen-SS during Charnwood. (*Canadian Army/Canadian National Archives*)

An infantryman hurries past a burning Sherman. Operation Charnwood, the infantry attack involving two British and one Canadian division, opened at 0420 on 8 July and it took two days of heavy fighting to drive the Germans from northern Caen and back across the Orne. (*Author's Collection*)

A Sherman edges past the same tank – crews had to be very alert at moments such as this in case enemy anti-tank guns or infantry with Panzerfausts were lying in ambush. (*Author's Collection*)

This Sherman belonged to the Canadian 2nd Armoured Brigade, which consisted of the 6th, 10th and 27th Armoured Regiments. Note the spare track links and wheels stored on the front of the hull to provide extra protection from enemy gunners. The British and Canadians deployed eight independent tank brigades in Normandy. (*Canadian Army/Canadian National Archives*)

A Canadian film unit were in the thick of it recording the Canadian Army's exploits. These men's mode of transport appears to be a Humber scout car or light reconnaissance vehicle, of which 3,600 were built during the war. (*Canadian Army/Canadian National Archives*)

In their moment of triumph three members of The Queen's Own Rifles of Canada, 8th Brigade, Canadian 3rd Infantry Division, pose by a Caen road sign on 9 July 1944. While the Allies took the city west of the Orne, because the bridges were down the Germans were able to hold onto the suburb of Vaucelles east of the river. (*Canadian Army/Canadian National Archives*)

Canadian troops examine captured German equipment: the weapon on the left is a German 75mm PaK 40 anti-tank gun, and the others are captured Soviet field pieces. The one on the right is the Soviet Model 1936/1939 76.2mm field gun, which was adopted into German service as an anti-tank gun using German ammunition. The gun behind it and the one behind the PaK 40 are Soviet Model 1938 122mm howitzers. The two self-propelled guns in the background are French artillery tractors converted to carry German howitzers – this type of conversion first saw action with Rommel in North Africa. (*Canadian Army/Canadian National Archives*)

A Crusader gun tractor pulling a 17-pounder anti-tank gun – this was a highly capable weapon but was never available in sufficient numbers during the Normandy campaign. The Gun Tractor Mk I used an obsolete Crusader II chassis and was widely used by the anti-tank regiments with the British armoured divisions in 1944. This one has been fitted with side extensions for deep wading during Operation Overlord. (*Author's Collection*)

This rather flat-looking vehicle is a British Morris Mk II light reconnaissance car and is quite rare as only 2,000 Mk Is and IIs were ever built. It normally had a three-man crew and was very cramped when closed up. This particular LRC is with the Canadian 3rd Infantry Division and was photographed just before Charnwood commenced. (*Canadian Army/Canadian National Archives*)

This Humber scout car clearly took a direct hit judging by the fact that its front wheels have been blown clean off and the wall behind has come down. It is believed to have belonged to the 7th Reconnaissance Regiment, Canadian 3rd Infantry Division. (*Canadian Army/Canadian National Archives*)

This American Sherman illustrates the perils facing Allied armour in Normandy's bombed-out towns and cites. The rubble impeded the way, clogging tracks, and every derelict building was a potential enemy strongpoint. This particular tank belonged to the 37th Tank Battalion, US 4th Armored Division and was photographed in late July. (*US Army/ NARA*)

Two Panzer Mk IV Ausf Js of SS-Panzer Regiment 2, 2nd SS Panzer Division Das Reich. These tanks were knocked out in a very early encounter with the US Army at St Fromond, just east of the N174 from Carentan to St Lô, on 9 July, following a clash with the US 30th Infantry Division. (*US Army/NARA*)

Chapter Seven

Galloping Goodwood

In order to gain time for Lieutenant-General Omar Bradley's US 1st Army, Montgomery decided to punch Operation Goodwood east of Caen. German defences in this area were very deep, as Rommel had expected this to be the region chosen by the Allies for their main breakout. However, he was unable to control the impending battle in person, because on 17 July his staff car was strafed and he was severely injured.

Montgomery's offensive, employing the 7th, 11th and Guards Armoured Divisions, was intended to seize the high ground south of Caen and stop the panzers switching west before the Americans launched Cobra. In the path of the British lay a series of stone-built villages amidst hedge-lined fields and orchards. Rommel and General Eberbach exploited these to the maximum. General von Obstfelder's 86th Corps consisted of three infantry divisions supported by the 21st and 1st SS Panzer Divisions, while the 12th SS at Lisieux constituted 1st SS Panzer Corps with a reserve. In addition Tigers of the 503rd and 101st SS heavy tank battalions were also available.

British intelligence greatly underestimated Rommel's defences, which were almost ten miles deep, supported by 230 panzers – although when other armoured fighting vehicles are included, this force totalled nearly 400. Rommel and Eberbach had built five defensive zones: the first consisted of the infantry, then sixty tanks from 21st Panzer and thirty-nine Tigers; there followed a chain of fortified villages and then the artillery on a gun line, including the Garcelles-Secqueville woods and the Bourguébus ridge supported by panzergrenadiers and Panther tanks from the 1st SS. The final zone comprised two battle groups from the 12th SS.

Rommel's gun line on the Bourguébus ridge included seventy-eight 88mm guns, 194 field guns, twelve heavy flak guns and 272 Nebelwerfer rocket launchers, although in reality much of this equipment was spread throughout the entire German defensive zone. Most of the 88mm anti-aircraft guns belonged to General Pickert's 3rd Flak Corps, which was under strict orders from Panzergruppe West to defend the Caen–Falaise road from air attack. Most of his guns were therefore to the south and east of Bourguébus, with air defence his priority.

Werner Kortenhaus recalled Goodwood's preliminary bombardment: 'It was a bomb carpet, ploughing up the ground. Among the thunder of the explosions we could hear the wounded scream and the insane howling of men who had been driven mad.' Panzer Mk IVs of 21st Panzer, along with Tiger tanks from the 503rd Heavy Tank Battalion, were caught in the Allied saturation bombing near Château de Manneville, sixteen miles east of Caen. The effects were devastating, with tanks simply flipped upside down like toys. From a force of about fifty tanks over half were lost and many others suffered mechanical problems.

Goodwood began at 0745 on the 18th and the 1st SS rushed north to join 21st Panzer to halt the attack on their left flank. About forty-six panzers were thrown into action against the British in the area of Bourguébus at 1620. Taking up positions on the ridge they inflicted heavy casualties on the British 7th and 11th Armoured Divisions, who received a very nasty surprise.

The British armour had 3,000 yards of open ground to cover before they reached the ridge marked by the villages of Bras, Hubert Folie and Bourgébus itself, all of which were German strongpoints. They got to within a few hundred yards before the enemy opened fire. A Squadron of the 3rd Battalion, Royal Tank Regiment swiftly lost thirty-four of its fifty-two tanks.

Just after 0930, determined to hold Cagny and the vital Bourguébus ridge, the Germans threw the 21st Panzer and 503rd Heavy Tank Battalion at the Guards and 11th Armoured Divisions with orders to regain the Caen–Troarn road. The Panthers of the 1st SS also rolled down from the ridge, driving the British back. In the process of trying to drive them to Caen–Troarn the two panzer divisions lost 109 tanks, while by the end of the first day the British had suffered 1,500 casualties and 200 tanks had been destroyed – all for the gain of just six miles beyond the Orne. The north–south line from Frénouville to Emiéville held and with the commitment of the 1st SS, Goodwood came to a grinding halt over the next few days.

Exhausted by the fighting, the panzers of 1st SS wanted to break off combat on the Bourguébus ridge, but their request was denied due to the activity of Allied fighter-bombers – presumably on the grounds that if they stayed in close proximity to the British then they were at less risk of air attack. Although German losses were relatively high, continuing to fight achieved the desired effect and the 11th Armoured Division lost 106 of its tanks. West of Cagny the Guards Armoured Division, having lost sixty tanks, was also held up.

Now that the Bourguébus ridge was such a bloody killing ground, when the panzergrenadiers from 1st SS moved up on the night of 18/19 July they must have been fearful that the Allied bombers would repeat the previous day's attack. The British brought up artillery on the 19th to cover the advancing tanks. However, the Northants Yeomanry veered towards Ifs, to the west of Bras, and were driven back towards Caen. At Bras the 1st SS defenders were not so lucky and were ejected at 1900 with the loss of a dozen self-propelled guns and many dead.

The 1st SS, 12th SS and 21st Panzer Divisions had effectively hemmed in Montgomery. By this point, the 1st SS had gathered seventy Panzer IVs and Panthers west of Bourguébus at Verrières on the far side of the Caen–Falaise road. A battle group from 2nd Panzer and the 272nd Infantry Divisions were also on the ridge, while the 116th Panzer Division was in the process of moving up behind the 12th SS.

Heavy rain and the actions of the 1st SS and 21st Panzer Divisions brought Goodwood to a halt on 20 July. The Churchill, Cromwell, Honey and Sherman tanks of the three British armoured divisions suffered extremely heavy casualties in terms of men and equipment. In just two days the British 2nd Army lost 413 tanks – some 36 per cent of its total tank strength. While Montgomery's losses in tanks were embarrassing, they could be easily replaced and he had drawn the panzers to him, although failure to break through Rommel's defences did not sit so well with the Allies.

British armour moving up for the attack: Operation Goodwood, conducted from 18–21 July 1944, east of Caen, was intended to assist with the capture of the city and pin down German forces prior to the American breakout. These Cromwell tanks belong to the 4th County of London Yeomanry (Sharpshooters), 7th Armoured Division, who had been mauled at Viller-Bocage. (*Author's Collection*)

A rather fearsome-looking Cromwell 'Prong' – the American Cullin Hedgerow Cutting Device was fitted to some Cromwell and Sherman tanks in June–August 1944 to help counter the restricting hedges and foliage of the Normandy bocage. This vehicle is actually an earlier Centaur III armed with a 75mm gun, making it equivalent to the Cromwell IV. (*Author's Collection*)

British mechanised infantry awaiting Monty's push south. Having just dug their protective slit trenches, they are taking the chance to catch up with the newspapers and mail from home. The vehicle is an American-supplied half-track, either the M2 or M3. (*Author's Collection*)

A British Sherman
Firefly poised for the
attack. Monty was
confident that his
three armoured
divisions (7th, 11th
and Guards) amassed
for Goodwood would
pierce the German
defences to the east of
Caen – however he
greatly underestimated
the depth and strength
of those defences.
(*Author's Collection*)

US Military Police,
supported by a US
Army M3 half-track
and an M5 light tank,
oversee German
prisoners being
marched to the rear.
While the US 1st
Army consolidated
its position,
Montgomery sought
to break out into the
open tank country
beyond Caen. (*US
Army/NARA*)

A US MP directs an M5 light tank bearing the name 'Concrete'. MPs played a vital role in helping keep the armour moving and avoiding traffic snarl-ups. (*US Army/NARA*)

A British or Canadian Sexton self-propelled gun (seen earlier in Chapter Two) laying down fire support. This was an Anglicised version of the American M7 Priest and was armed with the British 25-pounder field gun rather than the US 105mm howitzer. Built by the Canadians, the Sexton was deployed with the field regiments of the artillery divisions. Despite a heavy pounding much of the German defences remained intact when the tanks started to roll forward. (*Author's Collection*)

The RAF's Typhoons flew constant sorties, striking the panzer divisions stationed around Caen. The rockets being loaded onto this aircraft carried a 60lb explosive warhead. The fighter-bomber in the background is the Typhoon IB, flying with 609 Squadron, 123 Wing, which formed part of the RAF 2nd Tactical Air Force's No. 84 Group. (*Alan Jones Collection*)

A Typhoon taxiing to take off, ready to support Monty's armour. Initially the Normandy dust caused the aircraft's large air intake problems until rapid field modifications were made. (*Alan Jones Collection*)

This scene is typical of the sort of trail of devastation left by Allied fighter-bombers such as the Mustang, Thunderbolt and Typhoon when they found enemy armour exposed on the roads. This StuG III Ausf G has suffered a catastrophic hull explosion. The branches lying on the road were probably part of its camouflage. (*Author's Collection*)

This StuG III has thrown both tracks and become stranded. The lattice pattern on the hull is Zimmeritt anti-mine coating. During Goodwood the main German resistance centred on the vital Bourguébus ridge. (*US Army/NARA*)

French civilians get a closer look at a British carrier. (*US Army/NARA*)

The Panther was without doubt the best all-round panzer the Germans possessed. The third and final model, the Ausf G, seen here went into production in early 1944 and was used in equal numbers with the Ausf A in Normandy.

More debris of the Normandy battles. This Panther and the half-tracks of its supporting panzergrenadiers were caught in the open. Just behind the Panther is an M10 tank destroyer pushing through the shattered hedgerow. (*Author's Collection*)

A selection of Shermans armed with 75mm, 76mm and 105mm guns, plus a M32B1 Tank Recovery Vehicle waiting on a French quayside. Despite the British Army's major tank losses during Operation Goodwood, replacement armour was never a problem. (*US Army/NARA*)

An American Sherman and supporting infantry exercise caution amongst the Normandy hedgerows on the road to La Haye-du-Puits, north of Lessay. Once the Contentin peninsula was secured, making good their losses following the gruelling fight to Cherbourg took time and this held up the Americans' desire to break free of the Normandy bridgehead. (*US Army/NARA*)

GIs hitching a ride on the back of two Sherman tanks. While Monty's armour was slogging it out against Rommel's defences east of Caen the Americans were manoeuvring themselves into position ready to break the German defences in their sector. (*US Army/NARA*)

An American M10 festooned in sandbags gives an impressive display of its firepower – but like most Sherman tank derivatives, its armour remained far from satisfactory. (*US Army/NARA*)

In the right hands these German remote-control demolition vehicles could cause havoc. (*US Army/NARA*)

Chapter Eight

Cobra – Patton Breaks Out

The US 2nd Armored Division began to land on Omaha Beach just three days after D-Day, on 9 June. Its arrival did not go without mishap, as an LST struck a mine, losing sixty-six men, thirty-one tanks and fifteen other heavy vehicles. The division came ashore in three groups comprising Combat Commands A and B plus the support units. General Omar Bradley, commander of the US 1st Army, initially deployed them to the American left where they clashed with the 17th SS Panzergrenadiers at Carentan. This engagement gained them the German nickname 'Roosevelt's Butchers'. The 2nd Armored was then placed in reserve to await the rest of the units that still had to cross the English Channel. On 30 June, now under General Charles Corlett's 19th Corps, the division moved south-west of Bayeux to support the British flank.

For American armour the battle of the hedgerows ('bocage') was a bloody affair – for the infantry it was a gruelling ordeal. St Lô was scheduled to be captured on 11 June, but it did not fall until a month later on 18 July. Taking the town cost the 29th and 35th Infantry Divisions 5,000 causalities. To the west the Germans still held the Lessay–Periers road and were able to shell St Lô. The seventeen-day push seven miles west of the Vire, and ending up just four miles east of it, came at a cost of 40,000 American casualties, 90 per cent of whom were infantry. By mid-July the shortage of infantry meant that 25,000 reinforcements had to be demanded from America. Total German casualties by this time had risen to about 100,000.

While Montgomery was battling it out, Bradley's plan for Operation Cobra involved fifteen US divisions under Middleton's 8th Corps, Collins' 7th Corps and Corlett's 9th Corp respectively. Collins' 4th, 9th and 30th Infantry Divisions opened the attack, followed by the 1st Infantry, 2nd Armored and 3rd Armored. The intention was to break through and swing right, trapping five or six enemy divisions. As well as fighter-bomber and bomber support, a barrage was to be laid down by 1,000 guns. To fend off Cobra the Germans had eleven very weak divisions, only two of which were armoured (the Panzer Lehr and 2nd SS). The Panzer Lehr Division could muster barely 2,200 men and just forty-five operational armoured vehicles.

Hitler prevailed upon von Rundstedt and Rommel that they should wear the

Allies down, missing the point that this was the very thing happening to his panzer forces thanks to Mongomery's sledgehammer blows around Caen. After the 20 July bomb plot to assassinate him, Hitler took personal command of operations in the West. Following the initial American breakthrough he ordered six infantry divisions to replace the panzer divisions facing the British and Canadians so that they could retake Avranches. However, there were no mobile reserves to help 7th Army contain an Allied breakthrough and reinforcements lacked combat experience and were short of artillery and anti-tank weapons.

Frustrated with the dangerously confining bocage, which lined all of Normandy's roads and fields, the US Army deployed a simple but effective secret weapon for Cobra. Up until this point the hedgerows had served German defensive operations extremely well and they were proving lethal to American tanks: it seemed that behind every hedge lurked a panzer or an anti-tank gun. That was until 'Rhino' steel tusks were welded to the front of many American tanks.

While Sergeant Curtis C. Cullin of the 2nd Armored Division got the credit for devising a plough that effectively tore out the hedgerow's earth bank obstructing a tank, it was really a team effort. To be fair, by this stage many American armoured units were experimenting with field modifications that did not require the services of an armoured bulldozer or indeed a Sherman fitted with a bulldozer blade. The 17th Armored Engineer Battalion's 'tankdozers' (tanks fitted with bulldozer prows) had been deployed at Carentan as an ungainly solution.

Ironically the steel for the ploughs came from Rommel's beach obstacles. While the Rhinos were of great practical value the psychological impact was also immense because they encouraged American tankers to get off the roads and outflank the panzers. It would soon become the panzers' turn to become trapped in ever-greater numbers amongst the Normandy hedgerows.

Three US infantry divisions of Collins' 7th Corps were assigned the task of spearheading the breakout, drawing up on the Lessay–Periers–St Lô line. Initially scheduled for 24 July it had to be delayed due to the bad weather. The following day the Americans withdrew 1,200 yards, while bombers dropped over 4,000 tons of bombs on the German defences, in an area four miles long by one and a half miles wide, just south of the St Lô–Periers road.

Early on 25 July the assault troops moved off, only to meet determined German resistance. The 116th Panzer Division was thrown into the struggle to stabilise the German line. Two days later General Collins decided to launch his own armour into the thrust. The US 2nd Armoured Division lost one tank as they moved off and little serious opposition was met; 7th Corps armour then fanned out. Roncey, about six miles south-east of Coutances, was overrun by the US 7th Corps after they had trapped elements of the 2nd SS Panzer Division along with 122 panzers and 259 other vehicles.

It was not until Lieutenant-General George Patton's breakout, thirty miles further south at Avranches, a week after Cobra commenced that the pursuit really got underway. While Patton waited for his US 3rd Army to become operational, he took command of 8th Corps and drove southwards along the coast into Brittany, ready for the sweep into line for a thrust towards the Seine. He took Coutances and on 30 July the US 4th Armored Division, hurtling down from 8th Corps, seized Avranches on the Atlantic coast. The town's bridges were found to be intact.

On 1 August, ignoring Bradley's orders to secure a wide corridor, Patton squeezed six divisions down the coast through the gap at Avranches in twenty-two hours. He was now poised to sweep south-eastwards into the open plains in order to trap the Wehrmacht in north-western France. At this point, if not earlier, Hitler should have authorised a withdrawal beyond the Seine to the comparative safety of the German 15th Army. Instead he insisted that no inch of ground be given, denying his generals any initiative.

An overturned Flakpanzer 38(t) in the St Lô area. In Normandy this type of flakpanzer was in service with the 2nd, 9th and Panzer Lehr Divisions as well as the 1st SS. (*Author's Collection*)

As a GI dashes for cover a American M5 light tank engages enemy targets. Such armour received a mauling at the hands of the Waffen-SS. The 2nd SS Panzer Division Das Reich surprised the US 743rd Tank Battalion at le Dèsert on 9 July 1944, wreaking death and destruction. (*US Army/NARA*)

Two Ausf A Panthers at le Dèsert belonging to Panzer Lehr. They were put out of action by the US 9th Infantry Division, though the lack of visible damage indicates they may have been abandoned by their crews and later shunted off the road. (*US Army/NARA*)

A 2nd SS Panther Ausf A on fire at Sainteny, 8km south-west of Carentan. The GIs are believed to be from the US 4th Infantry Division and the photo was taken during 8–10 July. (*US Army/NARA*)

The roads to the north and east of St Lô were captured by 12 July and German prisoners grew in number. The town though did not fall until the 18th after a bitter eight-day siege that cost the Americans 5,000 casualties. It would be another week before they launched Operation Cobra, their breakout west of the town. (*US Army/NARA*)

US Military Police escorted P-47 Thunderbolt pilots to examine their handiwork on 19 July 1944. The two Panzer Lehr Panthers are both Ausf As; 215 seems intact and it is likely the crew fled in the face of American air attack. The other tank was clearly hit by bombs and rockets that blasted open the engine compartment and tore off the tracks. (*US Army/NARA*)

A group of American M8 armoured cars from the US 29th Infantry Division cause a slight road block in a French town on 19 July during the fighting for St Lô. (*US Army/NARA*)

Shermans of the US 5th Armored Division preparing for action. (*Author's Collection*)

An up-gunned M4A1 (76mm) leads a column of Shermans from the US 2nd Armored Division along a hedgerow. This variant only went into production in February 1944. The gun was also fitted to the M4A3 and the new horizontal volute spring suspension (HVSS) Sherman. Both the US 2nd and 3rd Armored Divisions were deployed to the west of St Lô with the US 7th Corps. (*US Army/NARA*)

Another American M5 light tank – note the prong on the front of the hull designed to dig up the Normandy hedgerows. (*US Army/NARA*)

The initial breakout assault on 25 July was preceded by a devastating bombing offensive, which left many of the defending formations stunned. The plan was for the US Army to strike south-west into Brittany and south-east towards Falaise and the River Seine. (*Author's Collection*)

Clearing rubble in Norman towns proved a problem. One solution was the Sherman M4A1 fitted with the M1 'dozer blade, seen here in action with the US 2nd Armored Division. These first appeared during the Italian campaign utilising parts from the D-8 'dozers – however the M1 'dozer blade was specially designed for the Sherman. The US Engineer Corps variant had their turrets removed. (*US Army/NARA*)

While Operation Cobra was devastating, these American tanks are taking no chances and have camouflaged themselves against enemy gunners. The vehicle in the foreground is an M8 Howitzer Motor Carriage, essentially the M5 light tank fitted with a 75mm pack howitzer (also seen on page 24). The Sherman behind it is an M4A1 armed with the 76mm gun. (*US Army/NARA*)

Men of the US 1st Infantry Division move around a knocked-out Sherman. (*US Army/NARA*)

More M8s from the 82nd Armored Reconnaissance Battalion, 2nd Armored Division, edge warily through deserted streets of St Sever Calvados in early August. (*US Army/NARA*)

Two knocked-out American M10s. (*US Army/NARA*)

A Sherman of the US 4th Armored Division in the Coutances area on 29 July, supporting troops from the US 90th Infantry Division. These divisions fought hard to drive back the 2nd SS Panzer Division and the 17th SS Panzergrenadier Division. (*US Army/NARA*)

The smashed remains of a Tiger tank are just visible in the second crater. (*US Army/NARA*)

Yet more detritus left behind by the brutal fighting in Normandy, consisting of an amphibious 4x4 Schimmwagen and a Marder self-propelled gun. In the Roncey pocket, created by Operation Cobra, where elements of Das Reich were caught, the Allies reaped a cruel harvest of tangled metal. (*US Army/NARA*)

A dead German lies by a disabled Sd Kfz 250 half-track from the 2nd Panzer Division. (*US Army/NARA*)

This still-smouldering Sherman from the 32nd Armored Regiment, Combat Command A, US 3rd Armored Division, seems to have come off worse in this face-off with a StuG III. The latter was from Sturmgeschütz Brigade 394, supporting the 116th Panzer Division. (*US Army/NARA*)

American M5s roll into Avranches five days after the launch of Operation Cobra, which opened the way for the American swing west into Brittany and east towards the Seine and Paris. (*US Army/NARA*)

Combat Command B of the US 4th Armored Division liberated Avranches on 31 July 1944. While the US 7th and 15th Corps swung east the 8th Corps headed west. Seen here are Shermans of the 68th Tank Battalion, US 6th Armored Division transiting Avranches en route to Brittany. (*US Army/NARA*)

German PoWs wait patiently behind the wire; many of them would end up in America. (*US Army/NARA*)

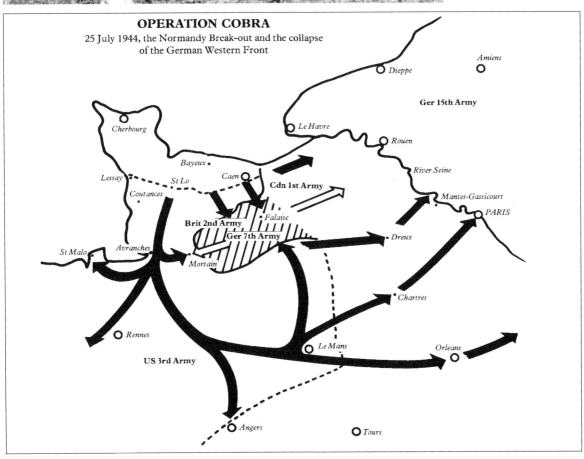

OPERATION COBRA

25 July 1944, the Normandy Break-out and the collapse of the German Western Front

Amiens

Dieppe

Ger 15th Army

Cherbourg

Le Havre

Rouen

Bayeux

Caen

River Seine

Lessay

St Lo

Coutances

Cdn 1st Army

Mantes-Gassicourt

PARIS

Falaise

Brit 2nd Army

Ger 7th Army

Dreux

St Malo

Avranches

Mortain

Chartres

Rennes

Le Mans

Orleans

US 3rd Army

Angers

Tours

Chapter Nine

Mortain – Hitler Strikes Back

Now in an effort to seal the American breakout, Hitler disastrously ordered a counter-attack to isolate Patton's 3rd Army. He wanted eight panzer divisions to assemble near Mortain, and to strike towards Avranches. In reality, Hitler's forces were simply driving themselves deeper into danger. When Captain Harry C. Butcher, Eisenhower's naval aide, pointed out to his boss that the Germans had about 500 tanks in the Mortain area, Eisenhower responded: 'We've got 3,500; what are we scared of?' The sentiment was right, but not the intelligence.

Panzergruppe West was renamed 5th Panzer Army on 5 August and given responsibility for 7th Army's right flank. General Eberbach considered a counter-attack a hopeless cause: his forces were too weak; Allied air power was too strong; and any success would be short-lived as it would be impossible to fend off the Americans once they caught their breath. In addition, supplying the four panzer divisions available for the attack would have to be conducted at night.

Nonetheless, Hitler ordered Operation Lüttich (Liège) to close the developing American breach. The panzers in Normandy were down from 1,400 tanks to 800, of which 120 were allotted to Liège (belonging to the 2nd and 116th Panzer Divisions as well as elements from Panzer Lehr and 2nd SS), supported by two infantry divisions. Only eighty panzers crossed the start line on 7 August, however; the tired Germans drove hard, taking Mortain and advancing seven miles before the US 30th Division held them until reinforcements arrived. Then, with the help of Allied air support, Hitler's counter-attack ran out of steam. RAF Typhoon fighter-bombers pounced on some 300 armoured vehicles, destroying eight, and other squadrons followed up to take their share of the kills. German troops dubbed it the 'Day of the Typhoon'.

Hitler's panzers got to within nine miles of Avranches but could get no further. The US 2nd Armored Division found itself slugging it out with depleted elements of 2nd Panzer, 2nd SS Panzer and Panzer Lehr in the vicinity of Barenton, and 116th Panzer around Vire. On 8 August 7th Army received orders to postpone the attack following a British breakthrough south of Caen, which had shaken the 5th Panzer Army.

Hitler demanded that the counter-attack in the American sector be renewed and instructed Eberbach to assume command of the newly activated Panzergruppe Eberbach on 10 August, while General 'Sepp' Dietrich took command of the 5th Panzer Army. The Allied pressure from both the American and British sectors was such that, despite the panzers' best efforts, the dam was about to burst in a very spectacular fashion.

In reality, for the renewed attack Eberbach could only gather 124 tanks, seventy-seven Panzer Mk IVs and forty-seven Panthers, roughly the same inadequate numbers that had been launched in the initial attack. His efforts, though, were stillborn once the Americans were south of Argentan. All thoughts of counter-attack were abandoned in favour of trying to extricate as many units as possible from the American, British, Canadian and Polish pincer movement now forming.

Eberbach blamed the failure of the German attack on Avranches squarely on the German High Command. Referring to the transfer of Panzergruppe West's armour to the 7th Army for the operation, he commented, 'The failure was caused by the fact that the panzer divisions of Panzergruppe West (5th Panzer Army), committed at the front, were not relieved by infantry divisions in due time. The Armed Forces High Command is to blame for this. It did not authorise CinC West to act freely, and delayed the transfer of the divisions.'

Patton, who was sweeping south of Le Mans, knew that if the Germans persisted with their attack then they would ultimately not be able to get away. Slowly but surely 7th Army and 5th Panzer Army were being wedged into a giant vice. In trying to stop Patton's tanks 9th Panzer Division was reduced to a dozen panzers.

The Allies could see their plans coming to fruition. The Canadians drove through the south of Caen and headed for Falaise, while the Americans sped eastwards, creating a gigantic trap. Montgomery ordered the Americans to make a long hook, in order to envelop as many of the enemy as possible and prevent them escaping over the Seine. However, the developing pocket could not be closed because the Germans dug in north of Falaise and the Canadian advance was slower than expected.

The US 5th Armored Division burst into Sees on the Orne on 12 August and headed north for Argentan, tightening the noose around over twenty German divisions. Trapped in the pocket were the cream of the German tank forces, including elements of the 9th, 21st, 116th, 2nd SS, 9th SS, 10th SS and 12th SS Panzer Divisions. By then 116th Panzer was down to only fifteen tanks, the 1st SS had just nineteen, the 10th SS eight and the 12th SS about twenty. The 116th Panzer Division tried to hold up the Americans, but the Germans lost 100 panzers that day. On 13 August 1st SS and 2nd Panzer were thrown piecemeal into the fight.

At Argentan, which lies south-east of Falaise, the Germans had just seventy tanks with which to fend off 300 American Shermans. General Bradley, fearing his troops might be trampled by the fleeing enemy, refrained from driving on to Falaise. This meant that the two German armies caught in the Falaise pocket were able to struggle eastwards for another week.

To the north the Germans held up the Canadian advance, known as Operation Tractable, for two days before they reached Falaise. At Falaise 1st SS was on its last legs and 12th SS only had fifteen tanks left.

An M5 Stuart tank of the 747th Tank Battalion on 19 July – like many under-armoured Allied tanks this has been piled up with sandbags in an effort to give its crew some extra protection. (*US Army/NARA*)

Roncey, about 10km to the south-east of Coutances, was in the sector overrun by the US 7th Corps' offensive west of St Lô on 25 July 1944. This row of Panzerjäger 38(t) Ausf Ms (Sd Kfz 138), armed with the 75mm PaK 40, is thought to be from the 2nd SS Panzer Division. (*US Army/NARA*)

The same scene only further up the road. The mangled remains of a Sd Kfz 7/2 mobile 37mm flak gun, the gun has been blown clean out of the vehicle and is in the road to the right. Behind is a Marder self-propelled gun. This equipment was photographed in the Roncey pocket, which had been created by Operation Cobra. (*US Army/NARA*)

Men of the 32nd Armored Regiment, US 3rd Armored Division take a breather at St Jean de Daye on 26 July 1944. The two visible Shermans are the up-gunned M4A1 (76mm), while a regular Sherman is parked between them. (*US Army/NARA*)

This American M5A1 of the 25th Cavalry Reconnaissance Squadron (Mechanised), US 4th Armored Division was photographed advancing through Coutances on 29 July. The tree trunk road block did little to delay their progress and the Germans had already departed. (*US Army/NARA*)

GIs from the US 8th Infantry Division plod past a German 88mm flak gun, which appears to have been abandoned while in transit. (*US Army/NARA*)

At the crossroads south-west of Notre-Dame-de-Cenilly Das Reich desperately fought to reach Percy on 28 July. One column of thirty panzers and 2,500 men, led by a Hummel self-propelled gun named 'Clausewitz' (seen here), became trapped with devastating results for the division. (*US Army/NARA*)

This way Avranches: photographed on 31 July, M8 armoured cars, an M3A1 half-track and jeeps from the 25th Cavalry Reconnaissance Squadron (Mechanised), US 4th Armored Division stop to accept a bottle of wine from a local. The German vehicle to the left belonged to the 2nd SS Panzer Division Das Reich. (*US Army/NARA*)

A very clear shot of the American M7 Priest, so called because of the pulpit-like weapons mount on the left-hand side of the hull, belonging to the 14th Armored Field Artillery Battalion, US 2nd Armored Division. This self-propelled gun first went into action with the British 8th Army in North Africa. (*US Army/NARA*)

Hitler's futile counter-attack towards Avranches at the end of the first week of August was stillborn as this knocked-out Panzer Mk IV and StuG IV testify. The latter was quite rare in Normandy, with only around 1,100 being produced, compared to 7,720 StuG III Ausf Gs. (*Normandie Mémoire Collection*)

German troops examine a destroyed Panzer Mk IV – judging by the level of damage, it had suffered a direct hit. (*Normandie Mémoire Collection*)

An American M3A1 half-track passes a disabled StuG III belonging to the Sturmgeshütz Brigade 394. (*US Army/NARA*)

This smashed Chenilette Renault 3IR tractor had been pressed into German service; quite a number in various guises were encountered by the Allies in Normandy. (*US Army/NARA*)

These GIs are examining a burning Sd Kfz 250 from the 2nd Panzer Division. The blast has blown the rear section, including the doors, clean off the vehicle. (*US Army/NARA*)

The camouflage did this Sd Kfz 251 little good. The dead panzergrenadier was unable to get clear of his vehicle. (*US Army/NARA*)

A dead crewman lies sprawled by his M10 – while this up-gunned Sherman was well armed, its open turret left the crew vulnerable to indirect fire from artillery and mortars (also seen on page 110). (*US Army/NARA*)

The Goliath (Sd Kfz 302) was remotely controlled and had a 60kg explosive charge. The larger Sd Kfz 301 was about the size of a British Bren gun carrier and carried a 500kg demolition charge. (*US Army/NARA*)

This MP is standing in front of a repossessed German Kettenrad tracked motor bike. (*US Army/NARA*)

Taken on 20 August, this shows GIs resting by an abandoned Panther Ausf A in Argentan, thought probably to belong to the 116th Panzer Division. (*US Army/NARA*)

Chapter Ten

Panzer Corridor of Death – Falaise

Hitler's position in France became impossible to maintain after 15 August 1944 when the Allies landed in the Riviera. By the end of the month Free French forces liberated Toulon and Marseilles, capturing 37,000 German troops. Hitler grudgingly agreed to let the German Army withdraw through the Argentan–Falaise gap on 16 August. The 2nd SS Panzer Corps (2nd SS, 9th SS, 12th SS and 21st Panzer Divisions) were to hold the northern flank against the British and Canadians; 47th Panzer Corps (2nd and 116th Panzer Divisions) were to defend the south against the Americans, while 7th Army and Panzer Group Eberbach/5th Panzer Army conducted a fighting retreat eastwards.

Patton's US 3rd Army and Crocker's British 1st Corps were slowly heading for each other and the Falaise pocket was steadily squeezed from all sides as the Germans fought to hold open the neck. By 17 August the pocket was only twenty miles wide by ten miles deep, containing about 100,000 men – remnants of fifteen divisions with elements from at least twelve others – all trying desperately to extricate themselves. The panzer divisions managed to hold the Americans and Canadians at bay, but the vast retreating columns were decimated by Allied fighter-bombers and artillery, the roads becoming choked with burnt-out vehicles, which added to the chaos.

Montgomery demanded the Trun–Chambois gap be closed and on 17 August issued orders stating, 'It is absolutely essential that both armoured divisions of 2nd Canadian Corps, i.e. 4th Canadian Armoured Division and 1st Polish Armoured Division, close the gap between 1st Canadian and 3rd US Army. 1st Polish Armoured Division must thrust past Trun and Chambois at all costs and as quickly as possible.' The Canadians and Poles were soon pressing hard on the Germans' flanks.

Canadian troops burst into Falaise on 16 August and three days later, supported by Sherman tanks, seized St Lambert-sur-Dives right in the path of the fleeing Germans. They held out for three days, withstanding efforts by the remains of 2nd Panzer to dislodge them. Germans escaping over the river came under constant fire and at one point the Canadians called artillery fire down onto their own positions in order to catch Germans fleeing through their positions. Canadian soldier Duncan Kyle recalled the carnage, 'Germans charred coal-black, looking like blackened tree trunks lay besides smoking vehicles. One didn't realise the obscene mess was human until it was poked at. I remember wishing the Germans didn't have to use so many horses. Seeing all those dead animals on their backs . . . The road to Falaise was nauseating. I felt like puking many times, what butchery. The air force did its job well.'

The escape route was just five miles wide by 19 August, though it would not be completely sealed for another two days, and the rapidly shrinking pocket measured just seven miles by six. Under pressure from German paratroops within the pocket the Polish tanks were forced to relinquish control of some of the roads and up to 4,000 paratroops, supported by just three panzers from 2nd SS, escaped. Outside the mouth of the pocket, on 20 August, the 2nd SS Panzer Corps attempted to reach the remnants of 7th Army, but with just twenty tanks they were unable to break through and the 9th SS were halted by the 2nd Polish Armoured Regiment.

Inside the corridor 2nd Panzer, with their remaining fifteen tanks, attacked towards Canadian-held St Lambert and found the bridge intact. Their commanding officer, General Freiherr Heinrich, recalled, 'The crossing of the Dives bridge was particularly horrible, the bodies of the dead, horses and vehicles and other equipment having been hurled from the bridge into the river formed a gruesome tangled mass.' The 10th SS and 116th Panzer managed to cross the River Dives via the St Lambert bridge and drove the encircling Allies away; the 116th escaped with just fifty vehicles.

The 9th SS tried to break through again on 21 August using two massive King Tiger tanks, but these were swiftly knocked out. The Allies began to mop up the remaining Germans trapped west of the Dives and about 18,000 men went into the 'bag' that day. In total the Germans lost 10,000 killed and 50,000 captured. They claimed that 40,000 troops escaped, although many of them were lost before they crossed the Seine.

When the Allies finally overran the panzers in the Falaise pocket the debris was quite phenomenal. In the American zone alone there were 5,000 German vehicles, 380 tanks and 160 self-propelled guns. The British, Canadian and Polish zones were littered with another 344 armoured vehicles. However, while the 2nd SS Panzer Corps lost 120 tanks during the counter-attack at Falaise, it managed to withdraw to fight another day.

The British 2nd Tactical Air Force claimed to have destroyed or damaged 190 tanks and 2,600 vehicles during its sorties over the Falaise battlefield. Subsequent analysis showed that RAF Typhoon rockets had not caused as much destruction as first thought or indeed claimed. It has been assessed that only about 100 armoured fighting vehicles had actually been knocked out in air strikes during the entire campaign. Nevertheless, German defences in Normandy lay in tatters.

Canadian troops fought their way into Falaise on 16 August 1944. On the 7th the British, Canadian and Polish armies had attacked along the Caen–Falaise road with Operation Totalise; this was followed by Operation Tractable on the 14th conducted by the Canadians. (*Author's Collection*)

German soldiers surrendering to the Canadian 4th Armoured Division at St Lambert-sur-Dives, which sits in the narrow valley between the villages of Trun to the north and Chambois to the south. Montgomery ordered this remaining escape route to be closed on 17 August. During the bitter two-day battle for the village the Germans lost 300 dead, 500 wounded and 2,100 captured, including some of the officers and men from 2nd Panzer Division, who laid down their arms under the watchful eye of Canadian Sherman tanks. At the same time the Americans were battling northwards towards Chambois. (*Canadian Army/Canadian National Archives*)

Another long file of German prisoners moving to the rear after surrendering to the Canadian Army. The need to close the trap on the Falaise pocket prompted the Canadians to launch Operation Tractable, though they were soon calling it 'The Mad Charge'. It commenced on 14 August 1944 and was opened by another massive attack by Bomber Command. The Canadian tanks were to charge in two simultaneous waves, 160 in the first and 90 in the second, followed by infantry in armoured carriers. (*Canadian Army/Canadian National Archive*)

Argyll and Sutherland Highlanders of Canada (Princess Louise's), 10th Infantry Brigade, Canadian 4th Armoured Division escort German PoWs to the rear at Trun on 19 August. They are driving what looks like a Stoewer R200 Spezial 4x4 Kfz 1, of which almost 13,000 were built during the war. (*Author's Collection*)

General Otto Elfeldt, commander of the German 84th Corps, was the most senior officer taken prisoner during the fighting to seal the Falaise gap. He was captured by the Polish 1st Armoured Division near Hill 113 on 20 August. (*US Army/NARA*)

US troops from the 80th Infantry Division, supported by the French 2nd Armoured Division, streamed into Argentan, south of Falaise, on 20 August. Argentan's capture helped seal the fate of those German forces still inside the Falaise pocket. (*US Army/NARA*)

A group of shots of the same Tiger II; on 21 August the 9th SS Panzer Division used two of these massive monsters to try and break out of the Falaise pocket. In the first shot a Staghound I has just driven by – built by the Americans, only 2,844 were produced and these were supplied exclusively to the British and Commonwealth armies. British crews found them too large and preferred their Daimler armoured cars. (*Canadian Army/Canadian National Archives*)

GIs from the US 90th Infantry Division pose with a Nazi flag. They are alongside a Panther from the 116th Panzer Division in the Chambois area. (*US Army/NARA*)

American troops examining the smoking remains of a German self-propelled gun Sd Kfz 75mm PaK 40/1 on a Lorraine Schlepper carrier, quite possibly from 21st Panzer Division. (*Author's Collection*)

A Panzer Mk IV lies abandoned amongst a column of wheeled vehicles including a 4x4 staff car and an ambulance. As all the tank's hatches have been left open it is quite possible that it ran out of fuel and its crew fled on foot. (*US Army/NARA*)

Another abandoned panzer, this time a Panther Ausf A which has clearly been hit on the right-hand side. This tank also belonged to the 116th Panzer Division and was probably knocked out by the US 3rd Armored Division. (*US Army/NARA*)

The final resting place of a young Waffen-SS panzergrenadier; the tube slung around his neck would have contained a replacement barrel for the MG42 machine gun. An ammunition belt is just visible beneath his left leg, whilst beside him is a pack of playing cards. (*US Army/NARA*)

Crouching Canadian troops watch the inferno of the Falaise gap as Allied fighter-bombers and guns bombard fleeing Germans trying to fight their way out of the pocket.
(*Canadian Army/Canadian National Archive*)

GIs processing some of the 50,000 German troops taken prisoner after the battle for Normandy was over. Note the variety of uniforms from a variety of units. (*US Army/NARA*)

Supreme Allied Commander General Dwight Eisenhower toured the Falaise battlefield after the pocket was overrun. He recalled that, 'It was literally possible to walk for hundreds of yards at a time, stepping on nothing but dead and decaying flesh.' The panzer is an overturned Tiger II. (*US Army/NARA*)

This German scrapyard includes two Panthers in the foreground, behind which are Panzer Mk IVs and a Marder self-propelled gun, as well as several Sd Kfz 251 half-tracks. (*US Army/NARA*)

This tank graveyard is near Isigny-sur-Mer in the American sector – it contains an array of Panzer Mk IVs, Panthers and StuGs. The two small vehicles in the foreground are requisitioned French Renault UE/AMX tractors used by the Germans as the Infanterie Schlepper UE 630(f). These particular ones have frames for the Wufrahmen 40 rocket launchers. Intriguingly the Sd Kfz half-track on the left has been painted with an American star. (*US Army/NARA*)

More captured German equipment at Isigny-sur-Mer including anti-aircraft, anti-tank and field guns. In the background are three 88mm flak guns, which tank crews greatly feared, and in the foreground are 20mm flak guns. In the centre on the right, the artillery pieces include an sFH18 150mm and leFH18 (M) and leFH18 105mm guns. On the left are half a dozen PaK 40 75mm anti-tank guns. (*US Army/NARA*)

The remains of a StuG III, the internal blast has lifted the gun housing off the chassis. (*Normandie Mémoire Collection*)

Chapter Eleven

Leclerc's Shermans

In the wake of D-Day the liberation of German-occupied Paris was always going to be controversial. In the event, it was French Sherman tanks that locked horns with the German defenders. The Free French 2nd Armoured Division, under General Leclerc, was transported from North Africa to England ready for the Normandy landings in April 1944. As if to drive home where the division was destined, all the tanks and vehicles had a map of France painted on them.

Leclerc's men were veterans of fighting in Libya and Tunisia. In the summer of 1943 Leclerc's force became known as the *2e Division Blindée* and was fully equipped along the lines of an American armoured division, with Sherman and Honey tanks, armoured cars, self-propelled guns and towed artillery. Its organisation included three tank regiments: *1er Regiment de Marche de Spahis Marocains, 12e Regiment de Chasseurs d'Afrique* and *501e Chars de Combat*.

Leclerc's armour came ashore on Utah Beach on 1 August 1944 and, along with three American divisions, formed the US Army's 15th Corps under General W.H. Haislip. The initial advance, covering seventy miles in four days, getting as far as Le Mans, was fairly uneventful. Then Patton's US 3rd Army swung north to help trap the retreating German Army in the Falaise pocket. Unfortunately, near Argentan Leclerc let his enthusiasm run away with him and his tanks clogged a road earmarked for petrol supplies. The ensuing chaos gave the Germans a much-needed breathing space. Tantalisingly, Leclerc and his men were just over 100 miles from the French capital.

Despite the loss of some tanks the division successfully established a bridgehead over the River Orne. Leclerc was now placed under the US 1st Army with 5th Corps under Major-General Gerow. General Charles de Gaulle, commander of the Free French forces, was concerned that the French Communists would liberate Paris and got an undertaking that Leclerc could enter the city. However, at this stage the Supreme Allied Commander, General Eisenhower, felt it best to bypass Paris to avoid being sucked into a costly fight with the German garrison. Once the Allies crossed the River Seine on 20 August Paris had lost all strategic importance.

Since early August Parisians had made the city ungovernable for the German garrison, though the resistance were under instructions from de Gaulle not to rise up until the arrival of Leclerc and the French 2nd Armoured Division. On 21 August Leclerc, ignoring orders, sent a reconnaissance group, consisting of ten tanks and ten armoured cars towards Paris. A furious Gerow ordered him to recall them, but Leclerc refused. However, the Communist resistance had already risen up a few days earlier, forcing Eisenhower's hand, and on 22 August he authorised the French 2nd Armoured and the US 4th Infantry Division to drive on Paris the following day.

The retreating German armed forces were in no position to assist in the defence of Paris – between 6 June and 19 August 1944 they had lost over 1,000 panzers and were now in a state of disarray. General Dietrich von Choltitz, the garrison commander, was under strict instructions to deny the Allies the city, even if it meant razing it to the ground. Choltitz fortunately was a cultured man who had no intention of going down in history as the one who torched Paris.

Leclerc's division, totalling 16,000 men, 4,200 vehicles and 200 Sherman tanks, converged on the city in three columns. The main attack was launched from the south with a feint from the south-west. Outlying German defences consisted of small numbers of panzers supported by anti-tank guns holed up in villages and at crossroads.

At Jouy-en-Josas three Shermans were lost in tank-to-tank engagements. Stiff resistance was also met at Longjumeau and Croix de Berny. German 88mm guns at Massy and Wissous accounted for more of Leclerc's tanks. Similarly an 88mm gun sited in the old prison at Fresnes, blocking the Paris road, held off three Shermans. The first was knocked out, but the second destroyed the gun and the third ran over it. The French lost another four tanks to German anti-tank guns as they tried to outflank Fresnes. The push on Paris cost the division seventy-one killed, 225 wounded, with thirty-five tanks, six self-propelled guns and eleven assorted vehicles disabled or destroyed.

On the evening of 24 August a Free French patrol slipped into the city. Three light tanks, four armoured vehicles and half a dozen half-tracks entered Paris through the Porte Gentilly. By nightfall the tanks were within a few hundred yards of Choltitz' HQ. The next day, as the division entered in force, its tanks were mobbed by cheering crowds as they crossed the Seine bridges.

During five hours of fighting to clear the German defenders from the Foreign Office building on the Quai d'Orsay a Sherman tank was lost. At the Arc de Triomphe a French tank silenced its German counterpart at a range of 1,800 metres. Unfortunately Choltitz felt honour dictated that he put up at least token resistance before surrendering. Three Shermans were lost after they drove into the grounds of Place de la Concorde with their turret hatches open and each received a German grenade.

When the German garrison finally capitulated it was Leclerc's signature that was on the surrender document. Triumphantly de Gaulle and Leclerc walked from the Arc de Triomphe to Notre Dame with the division proudly lining the route. There were still

2,000 Germans in Paris when the parade took place and fighting was still going on. Gerow ordered Leclerc to clear the Germans from the northern suburbs while de Gaulle wanted to keep the division in Paris to counter the Communists. The liberation cost the French 2nd Armoured Division 130 dead and 319 wounded.

Following the closure of the Falaise gap General Charles de Gaulle, commander of the Free French forces, was determined that the tanks of the French 2nd Armoured Division would get the honour of liberating Paris. On 19 August almost all of the Parisian police staged a general uprising, stealing the thunder of the local Communist resistance. The Germans counter-attacked the Police Prefecture building using tanks, but fortunately withdrew before things turned really ugly. The resistance also liberated the Palais de Justice and Hôtel de Ville and barricades were erected throughout the capital. (*Author's Collection*)

The Free French 2nd Armoured Division was understandably disappointed not to form one of the spearhead divisions on D-Day. Instead it acted as one of the follow-up formations coming ashore on Utah Beach on 1 August 1944. Seen here are two of the division's Shermans being landed by US *LST 517. (US Army/NARA)*

The massed strength of one of General Leclerc's tank regiments – the *12e Regiment de Chasseurs d'Afrique*. Organised along American lines, French armoured divisions contained three armoured regiments, each with an HQ squadron, a squadron of seventeen M5 light tanks and three squadrons each of seventeen Shermans (each squadron had three platoons of five tanks each). (*US Army/NARA*)

General Leclerc chats with a Sherman tank crew from the *501e Chars de Combat* armoured regiment. Leclerc was a veteran of the battles fought in North Africa and inspired great loyalty amongst his men. (*US Army/NARA*)

An M3A3 Stuart light tank from the French 2nd Armoured Division is greeted by French well-wishers en route to the front. Much of its equipment initially came from the US 2nd Armored Division following the Allied landings in French North Africa. (*US Army/NARA*)

General Leclerc found himself in a difficult position, being under the command of Major-General Gerow's US 5th Corps but also answering directly to General de Gaulle. Being a pragmatic Frenchman, Leclerc knew where his first loyalties lay. Unfortunately, near Argentan Leclerc let his enthusiasm run away with him and his tanks clogged a road earmarked for petrol supplies. The ensuing chaos gave the Germans a much-needed breathing space. Tantalisingly, Leclerc and his men were just over 100 miles from the French capital. (*US Army/NARA*)

French resistance fighters lead a female collaborator past an American Sherman to an uncertain fate. The FFI or French Forces of the Interior, which encompassed the resistance, came under General Koenig, who also answered to de Gaulle. (*US Army/NARA*)

Leclerc's corps commander, General Gerow, complained bitterly that French troops were celebrating at every town and village, with predictable results. Such euphoria though was perhaps understandable. (*Author's Collection*)

148

On the evening of 24 August, just three days after the Falaise pocket had been overrun, elements of the French 2nd Armoured Division slipped into Paris. Here a column of French M3A3 or M5A1 Stuart light tanks roll into the city. The M3 light tank had been declared obsolete by the US Army in 1943, but continued to be used by the other Allies. (*Author's Collection*)

A Free French M10 tank destroyer engages enemy snipers with its machine gun. The German commandant initially refused to surrender, resulting in needless bloodshed – ultimately German resistance was futile. (*Author's Collection*)

Cheering crowds impede Leclerc's M4 Sherman tanks along the Avenue d'Orléans. From a force of about 200 Shermans Leclerc lost forty liberating the French capital: battles at German strongpoints on the outskirts of the city accounted for most of them. (*Author's Collection*)

A French M3 half-track personnel carrier and a lorry nudge their way through jubilant crowds. (*Author's Collection*)

A Free French 57mm M1 anti-tank gun (this was the American version of the British 6-pounder) and its M2 half-track prime mover draw admiring glances from local Parisians. The German garrison had very few tanks, and those that it did have were dealt with swiftly. (*Author's Collection*)

One of the Free French 2nd Armoured Division's Shermans being mobbed on the streets of Paris outside the Hôtel de Ville, which had already been liberated by the FFI. (*Author's Collection*)

FFI fighters inspect a column of Leclerc's armour beneath Notre Dame. They felt that they should take the credit for liberating Paris, not the French 2nd Armoured Division. They are clambering over an M3 light tank; behind it is an M3A3 Sherman armed with the 76mm gun, and the latter has at least another six Shermans behind it. (*Author's Collection*)

The captured military governor of Paris, General Dietrich von Choltitz, was described by Field Marshal von Rundtsedt as 'decent but stupid'. Earlier he had served as a corps commander in Normandy but his handling of the Panzer Lehr Division had been decidedly lacklustre. In Paris his garrison amounted to 10,000 men, supported by twenty, mostly elderly, French tanks and 256 flak guns of various calibre. The force was about adequate to contain any insurrection, but nothing else. (*Author's Collection*)

When von Choltitz surrendered on 25 August there were still 2,000 German troops in the city and fighting continued in the suburbs. These men, though, have clearly had enough. (*Author's Collection*)

A US Army M8 six-wheeled armoured car (known as the Greyhound in British service) beneath the iconic Arc de Triomphe. This vehicle is presumably from the US 4th Infantry Division. General de Gaulle took this route to Notre Dame on 26 August, ensuring that he and Leclerc's Shermans were perceived as the saviours of Paris. (*US Army/NARA*)

Generals de Gaulle and Leclerc (centre and left respectively) inspecting the French 2nd Armoured Division. Their insistence on holding a victory parade with their troops proved an embarrassment to the other Allies, who wanted them to concentrate on their military role. (*Author's Collection*)

The faces of these Parisians say it all. Thanks to the actions of Leclerc's Shermans de Gaulle's profile not only ensured that he took credit for liberating Paris, but also subsequently secured him the French presidency. (*Author's Collection*)

A fitting resting place for one of Leclerc's Shermans, as a memorial to the D-Day landings. (*Author's Collection*)

Early September and FFI fighters hitch a lift with the tanks of the US 3rd Armored Division as it liberates yet another French village. Quite what the GIs made of this rat-tag army is another matter. (*US Army/NARA*)

Chapter Twelve

Rouen and the Great Escape

While the destruction of the 5th Panzer Army and the 7th Army in the Falaise pocket seemed a deathblow from which Hitler could never recover, crucially numerous units escaped. Altogether there were about 250,000 German troops and 250 panzers still west of the Seine, consisting of men outside the pocket, those who had managed to get out of the pocket and units withdrawing from the south of France, all streaming eastwards in retreat. In mid-August Hitler, finally grasping the gravity of the situation, had ordered all non-combatant troops in western and southern France to commence withdrawing beyond the Seine.

The remains of the 5th Panzer Army took command of the entire sector west of the Seine, ordering that Elbeuf, lying on a huge westward-facing loop in the river south of Rouen, should be held. The remnants of three panzer divisions (2nd SS, 21st and 116th Panzer) were melded into Group Schwerin with about twenty battle-worthy tanks and assault guns.

On the night of the 23/24 August 21st Panzer and 2nd SS moved to reinforce the eastern flank of 5th Panzer Army, between the Seine and the Risle, in an effort to protect the vital crossings near Rouen. The 21st Panzer was subordinate to 116th Panzer, while 2nd SS were to hold blocking positions south and south-east of Elbeuf. By the evening of the 24th a line had been established between Elbeuf and the Risle north of Brionne. The withdrawing 9th SS were also ordered to join Group Schwerin.

Field Marshal Model instructed 'Sepp' Dietrich to counter-attack with his panzer divisions and a few weak panzergrenadier units; about thirty panzers were launched into a feeble attack that was swiftly halted. This was repeated on the 24th with similar results. In the meantime the exhausted German 7th Army, no longer capable of directing anything, was ordered to collect all available infantry units beyond the Seine.

By 25 August, as the retreat got underway, the 5th Panzer Army was able to muster just 18,000 men, forty-two tanks and assault guns and 314 guns – essentially a single panzer division. These forces were pulled back to the Seine bridgehead formed by three large river loops to protect the crossings at Caudebec-en-Caux, Duclair, Elbeuf and Rouen.

Model's men did all they could to hold up the US 2nd Armored Division's attempt to cross the River Avre at Verneuil. Suffering heavy casualties the Americans then crossed upstream, swinging north towards Elbeuf. They penetrated the town on 24 August but the following morning were expelled by the 2nd SS. German resistance was so fierce that one American column attacking from the south-east was cut off for two days and nights.

Complete withdrawal across the Seine became an imperative and Model gave the order. Priority was given to the armoured fighting vehicles, then motorised and finally horse-drawn transport. Model's troops made for the crossings at Elbeuf, Oissel and Rouen, which were under constant air attack. The key crossing point was at Rouen, so holding the wooded banks at the bulge in the river became vital, although with the river unfordable and with all the bridges down they had to rely on boats and rafts.

The pontoon bridge at Rouen could only take wheeled vehicles and the bridge at Oissel – the original having been destroyed in May – was likewise makeshift. Many surviving panzers and other vehicles that had been so painstakingly coaxed eastwards were abandoned on the dockside. On the 25th bombers attacked the German transport amassed on the quayside twice: the following day the fires were still raging both sides of the river.

The 116th Panzer and a battle group from the 2nd SS were given the task of holding the Americans at bay at Elbeuf, but on 26 August 2nd Armoured overran the town's southern outskirts. Having kept the Americans pinned down, 116th withdrew at midnight under the cover of fog and rain, and members of the 2nd SS escaped by swimming across the river. The 10th SS crossed at Oissel on 25–27 August by means of two bridges they had seized, selfishly fending off attempts by other retreating units to use them until all their own troops had crossed.

While the Canadian 3rd Armoured Division crossed at Elbeuf, the Canadian 2nd Infantry Division pushed through Forêt de la Londe, whose wooded hills stretched northwards all the way to Rouen. They suffered almost 600 casualties in three days of bitter fighting. Model decided that the 7th Army would cover the withdrawal of 5th Panzer Army towards Arras, north-east of Amiens and behind the safety of the Somme.

At Amiens 'Sepp' Dietrich was supposed to hand command of the 5th Panzer Army back to Eberbach on the afternoon of the 31st. Dietrich left early and Eberbach, commanding 7th Army, and his staff were surprised by British tanks rumbling into their midst. They were compelled to surrender: Eberbach's only reserves were just five Tiger tanks and they could achieve little in the face of the British 11th Armoured Division.

Partly thanks to the rearguard action at Rouen there was no second Falaise pocket; frustratingly for the Allies, the bulk of those German forces west of the Seine – 240,000 troops, 30,000 vehicles and 135 panzers – escaped over the river. After Falaise German armoured vehicle losses were modest considering the rapidity of the

Allies' advance – only sixty panzers and 250 other armoured vehicles were left on the west bank and about 10,000 troops were captured.

Much heated debate has raged about the effectiveness and employment of Hitler's panzers in Normandy, though it was actually the numerically superior German infantry divisions that bore the brunt of the fighting. The failure of the panzers to launch a decisive counter-stroke and their subsequent defeat has been blamed on a muddled chain of command, inertia, Hitler's intransigence over giving up ground and the Allies' superiority on the ground, in the air and at sea.

Allied armour, though, did not have it all its own way. While the Allies sought to counter Hitler's technological lead on land, sea and air at every single stage of the war, their failure to develop a war-winning battle tank was a glaring omission that even British Prime Minister Winston Churchill sought to hide from the general public lest it affect morale.

Despite extensive combat experience with the American and British armies in North Africa, Sicily and Italy, by 1944, for a variety of reasons, the Americans had failed to develop a worthy successor to the M4 Sherman, which meant that the Allies had to rely on numbers rather than quality. This critical failure was a key factor in the Germans being able to hold on for so long in Normandy. It also explains how Montgomery was able to shrug off the loss of two entire divisions' worth of tanks following Operation Goodwood.

Paris after the liberation – in reality Rouen, not the French capital, proved pivotal in the battle for the Seine. Although the Americans established a bridgehead over the Seine, west of Paris, on 20 August – just as the Falaise gap was sealed – German resistance on the west bank held out for another week. While the Allies were battling to liberate Paris the remaining panzers fought a desperate rearguard action against the British and Canadians to the north-west in the Rouen and Elbeuf area in an effort to keep four vital river crossings open. (*US Army/NARA*)

The American architects of the southern flank of the Falaise salient: (left to right) Generals Bradley, Gerow, Eisenhower and Collins. Bradley's decision to halt the US 15th Corps' tanks at Argentan to avoid 'friendly fire' incidents partly ensured that the Falaise pocket was not sealed quickly enough. (*US Army/NARA*)

Apprehensive-looking German PoWs. Once the Falaise gap was closed off, all eyes were on the Seine and the city of Rouen as the remaining German forces in France sought to escape wider encirclement. (*Author's Collection*)

More detritus of war: GIs examine abandoned German artillery. Visible are four 150mm field guns, a PaK 43 88mm anti-tank gun and a FlaK 36 88mm anti-aircraft gun. Those German units that escaped Falaise abandoned most of their heavy equipment around the Seine. (*Author's Collection*)

This smashed King Tiger (Tiger II) was a victim of the Normandy battles and, judging by the vast crater it is lying in, was a victim of the RAF's bombers. Tigers were known to be flipped over in such attacks, leaving the crews trapped inside. (*Author's Collection*)

Another discarded PaK 43: the anti-tank version of the famous FlaK 36. This was by far the best tank killer that the German Army possessed and guns such as these helped take a heavy toll on Monty's armour during his Goodwood offensive. However, this original model PaK 43 had a complex mounting and was slow to manufacture, and as a result the cheap and cheerful PaK 43/1 appeared, using the wheels from the sFH18 150mm and the trail legs from the leFH18 105mm. (*Author's Collection*)

While those panzer troops who escaped or avoided the chaos and carnage of Falaise attempted to coax their tanks to the Seine, many such as this King Tiger (seen earlier) were simply abandoned at the roadside for the want of fuel. The scorching on the turret suggests that the crew set it on fire. (*Canadian Army/Canadian National Archives*)

If Falaise saw the end of German horse-drawn transport, then Rouen and the western banks of the Seine saw the end of the German Army's motor transport. For about two miles along the river there was a mass of burnt-out and bombed vehicles, amongst which lay 2,000 dead. (*Author's Collection*)

Cast hull M4A1 Shermans shelling German positions. The US 5th Armored Division found itself up against General Höcker's 17th Luftwaffe Field Division just as the Falaise pocket was forming. Afterwards Höcker's command played a role in the rearguard at Elbeuf, fighting the Canadian 3rd and Polish 1st Armoured Divisions. (*US Army/NARA*)

The crew of a highly camouflaged M10 tank destroyer take a rest break. Despite the American and British Armies being hot on their heels the Germans managed to conduct a successful rearguard action with limited numbers of panzers.

A column of smouldering Sd Kfz 251 half-track armoured personnel carriers. The SS-Panzergrenadier regiments of the 2nd SS Panzer Division Das Reich had almost 260 such APCs. Although the division avoided being trapped it still had to abandon thirty panzers around Falaise because of a lack of fuel and spares. (*US Army/NARA*)

British troops finally crossing the Seine by pontoon bridge; once the Allies were over the river and in Paris the German position at Rouen became increasingly untenable. In both shots a carrier can be seen halfway over the bridge. (*Author's Collection*)

British carriers and tanks pushing across the Somme Valley. The lead tank appears to be a Cromwell or Centaur OP command tank. In Normandy such dust normally sparked heavy shelling from the enemy, but by this stage the Germans were in full flight. The British entered Arras on 1 September 1944. (*Author's Collection*)

A Sherman by the name of 'Hurricane' from the US 2nd Armored Division (last seen on page 33) gets a new engine courtesy of the 2nd Armoured Ordnance Battalion. A key factor with Allied armoured units was the logistical support. Mechanics were vital in keeping the tanks in the field; the British learned the hard way in North Africa that battlefield salvage could often redeem many lost tanks. (*US Army/NARA*)

A knocked-out StuG III (seen earlier) somewhere in France. Only sixty panzers and 250 other armoured fighting vehicles were left on the west bank of the Seine (largely for the want of fuel or viable crossings). In total the Germans left behind 1,500 tanks and assault guns in Normandy. (*Normandie Mémoire Collection*)

German troops go into captivity with Patton's 8th Corps in late July. Despite the Allies' best efforts, their sweep to the Seine did not achieve the same success as Falaise. Only 10,000 Germans were captured during this follow-up operation and almost a quarter of a million enemy troops escaped to fight another day. (*US Army/NARA*)